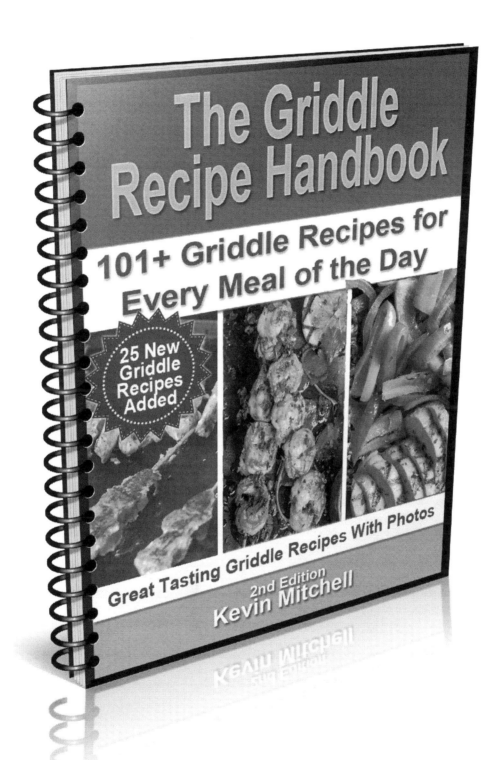

The Griddle Recipe Handbook

Contents

Introduction 6
About this Griddling Recipe Cookbook: 6
Insider's Secrets to Griddling, ... 7
    Cooking Oils 8
    Preheating Your Griddle 9
    Best Temperatures for Cooking 9
    Best Temperature for a Variety of Food Types: 10
    Basting Covers 11
    Cast Iron Grill Press 12
    Cooling Racks 12
    Spatulas, Egg Rings, Scrapers and More… 13
Appetizers 14
    Mozzarella Sticks Recipe 14
        Using Frozen Mozzarella Cheese Sticks: 14
    Pesto Sauce with Rice Crackers Recipe 15
    Super Stuffed Potato Skins 16
    Super Cheesy and Easy Potato Wedges 17
    Cheese and Bacon Stuffed Mini Sweet Peppers 18
    Stuffed Bell Peppers with Cheese and Homemade Crotons 19
    Recipe #2: Stuffed Bell Peppers with Cheese, Hamburger and Rice. 19
    Bacon Jalapeño Cheese Ball Appetizer 20
    Bacon-Wrapped Water Chestnuts with Spicy Mustard Dip 21
    Bruschetta with Mushrooms & Herbed Cheese 22
    Blackened Broccoli Side Dish 23
    Portobello and Sage-Stuffed Acorn Squash 24
Breakfast Recipes 25
    Hard Boiled Eggs 25
    Inside Out Scotch Eggs 26
    Traditional Scotch Eggs 26
    Bell Pepper & Onion Omelet 27
    Chicken & Ham Fried Eggs 28

The Griddle Recipe Handbook

- Chopped Tomatoes & Scrambled Eggs 29
- Sausage, Egg and Cheese Sandwich 30
- Open-Faced Egg Sandwich 30
- Pumpkin Spice Pancakes 31
- Flourless Protein Pancakes 32
- Coconut Flour Pancakes 33
- Easy Parmesan Breakfast Potatoes 34

Lunch – Wraps, Sandwiches and More Recipes 35
- Chicken BBQ Wrap Recipe 35
- Deluxe Griddled Chicken Sandwiches 36
- Hawaiian Ham & Pineapple Grilled Cheese Sandwich Recipe 37
- Amazing Grilled Cheese Crab and Lobster Sandwich 38
- Honey Cheddar Sourdough Grilled Cheese Recipe 39
- Spinach & Soy Sauce Turkey Wraps 40
- Chunky Chicken Salad Lettuce Wraps 41
- Taco-Stuffed Portobello Mushroom Caps 42
- Super Easy Tri-Color Griddled Carrots 44
- Mediterranean-Inspired Stuffed Portobello Mushrooms 45
- Warm Turkey, Pesto and Provolone Sandwich 46

Dessert and Snack Recipes 47
- Coconut Balls – Cardamom 48
- Crispy Chocolate Covered Banana Treats Recipe 49
- Rum Glazed Bananas – An Adult Treat 50
- Blueberries & Honey Roasted Almonds 51
- Dark Chocolate Brazil Nuts 52
- Salt & Pepper Pumpkin Seeds 53
- Maple Bacon Griddled Pumpkin 54

Dinner Recipes – Chicken, Pork and Steak 55
- Lemon Pepper Marinated Pork 55
- Lemon Pepper Marinated Pork 56
- Honey Paprika Chicken Tenders Recipe 57
- Sizzling Chicken Mushroom Recipe 58

The Griddle Recipe Handbook

- Southern Fried Turkey Strips with Stuffed Mushrooms 59
- Orange-Cranberry Bone-In Chicken Breasts 60
- Honey Applesauce Pork Roast 61
- Steak 62
- Herb-Rubbed, Bone-In Pork Chops 63
- Maple-Balsamic Boneless Pork Chops 64

Kebab Recipes 65
- Chicken & Onion Kebabs 66
- Pork & Red Pepper Kebabs 67
- Monkfish & Mushroom Kebabs 68
- Vegetable Kebabs 69
- Healthy Fruit Kebabs 70

Refreshing Drink Recipes 71
- Watermelon Mint Lemonade 71
- Sparkling Blackberry Basil Cocktail 72
- Passion Tea Lemonade 73
- Cherry and Mint Fizz 74
- Pink Grapefruit Martini – Adults Only 75
- Raspberry Margarita 76

Asian Recipes 77
- Beef Honey Curry Stir Fry Recipe 77
- Smoked Pork Sausage Hakka Noodles Recipe 78
- Asian Style Beef Broccoli Recipe 79
- Exotic Asian Pork Burger Recipe 80
- Oriental Glazed Pork 81
- Pot Stickers 82
- Sweet & Sour Pork Chops with Peppers & Pineapple 83

How to Make Super Juicy and Flavorful Hamburgers 84
- Super Juicy Grilled Burgers with Blue Cheese and Avocado 85
- Chicken Burgers 86
- Super Duper Juicy Hamburgers 87
- Lamb Burgers 88

The Griddle Recipe Handbook

- Salmon Burgers 89
- Vegetable Burgers 90
- Tex Mex Sliders 91
- Turkey Spinach Burgers 92

Mexican Recipes 93
- Goat Cheese Quesadilla Recipe 93
- Chimichangas (Shredded Beef) 94
- Ancho Chicken Quesadillas 95
- Easy Chicken Quesadillas 96
- Tequila Lime Beef Tacos 97

Pizza Recipes 98
- BBQ Chicken Pizza 98
- Breakfast Pizza 99
- Caprese Pizza with Tortilla Crust 100
- Oregano Pizza Crust Recipe 101

Seafood Recipes 102
- Sausage & Shrimp Recipe 102
- Smoked Salmon Rollups Recipe 103
- Warm Garlic-Parmesan Shrimp 104
- Lemon-Garlic Jumbo Shrimp 105
- Grilled Tequila Shrimp 106
- Orange Roughie with Oven-Roasted Tomatoes 107
- Steamed Citrusy Orange Roughie 108
- Coconut Shrimp with Avocado-Lime Dip 109
- Citrus Jumbo Scallops 110

Tofu Recipes 111
- Crispy Buffalo Tofu Fingers 111
- Garlic Tofu and Beans Stir Fry 112
- Korean Spicy Braised Tofu 113
- Teriyaki Tofu Steaks 114

Salad Recipes 115
- Caesar Salad 115

The Griddle Recipe Handbook

- Coleslaw 116
- Green Pea Salad 117
- Ranch Salad 118
- Sweet Potato Salad 119
- Marinated Strip Steak Salad with Creamy Blue Cheese Dressing 120

Great Tasting Salad Dressings 122
- Caesar Dressing 122
- Ranch Dressing 123
- Blue Cheese Dressing 124
- Tomato Ketchup 125

Sausage Recipes 126
- Pork Sausages 127
- Beef Sausages 128
- Lamb Sausages 129
- Turkey Sausages 130
- Vegetable Sausages 131

Additional Resources: 132

The Griddle Recipe Handbook

Introduction

About this Griddling Recipe Cookbook:

Over 101+ great tasting griddle recipes for any meal of the day. You'll enjoy all the recipes included in this one-of-a-kind book for flat top cooking. This book includes recipes for breakfast, lunch, dinner, salads and even desserts.

Nothing is better than heating up the flat top griddle and grilling your own tasty masterpieces. This book will have you grill'n great tasting recipes from the very day you grab your own copy. With over 101+ great tasting, flat top grill'n recipes to choose from, you'll soon be looking for any reason to get yourself in front of your flat top grill.

You'll be grill'n up yummy recipes for friends, family and co-workers for every meal of the day. Check out just a few of the recipes in this book:

- Citrus Jumbo Shrimp
- Hard Boiled Eggs
- Super Stuffed Potato Skins
- Steak
- Traditional Scotch Eggs
- Coconut Balls
- Rum-Glazed Bananas
- Mozzarella Sticks
- BBQ Chicken Pizza
- Citrus Jumbo Scallops
- Tequila Lime Beef Tacos
- And More...

Each recipe was created specifically for flat top griddle cooking.

Sincerely,

Kevin Mitchell

The Griddle Recipe Handbook

Insider's Secrets to Griddling,

Nothing is better than cooking outdoors, especially on your own flat top griddle. Like many of you, before getting my flat top griddle, I cooked on either a propane grill or a charcoal grill.

Now I do most of my cooking on my flat top. I simply love it. It's simple to cook on, it's easy to clean and best of all, the more you use it, the more the flavors get seared into the griddle top.

No matter if I am cooking breakfast, lunch, dinner or dessert, the food comes off delicious. With that being said, cooking on a flat top griddle is a little different than using a propane or charcoal grill. The reason is flat top cooking is so flexible.

In this section, I would like to share with you the secrets I have learned over the years. I wish I had this inside information when I first bought my flat top griddle several years ago. I wouldn't have overcooked and outright burnt so many recipes. ☐

Feel free to use this section as a reference point to help you make the best recipes on your own griddle.

The Griddle Recipe Handbook

Cooking Oils

When cooking on a griddle, you'll be using oils. Here are the top choices many griddle masters use:

- Avocado oil
- Butter
- Coconut oil
- Grapeseed oil
- Olive oil
- Peanut oil
- Sesame oil
- Vegetable oil

Since you will be using a lot of oil, the healthy oils may be the ones you may want to consider using consistently. These include coconut, flaxseed or olive oil. The cheaper alternatives are canola or soybean oil. However, like any grill master, you will ultimately be using the oil that is most flavorful to you and your griddling style.

The best way to use oil is with a <u>simple squeeze bottle</u>. You'll probably want to have different bottles for type of oil. You will also want to have a bottle for water, too. Like oil, water it vital to cooking on a flat top. Not only will you use plenty of water to clean you're the surface after each use, but it also provides the benefit of steam for certain recipes. Several of the recipes in this book use steam to help cook the food.

The Griddle Recipe Handbook

Preheating Your Griddle

When preheating, preheat your griddle on "medium-low" to "medium" for best results. The reason is high heat can burn the oil to the surface of your griddle.

Best Temperatures for Cooking

High, medium or low? Which is the best temperature for cooking? As with all cooking, it depends on the food and how you want it cooked. Thankfully, flat tops have simple dials to let you basically know the broad temperature of the different heat zones for your griddle. Many of the recipes in this book, use heat ranging from medium to high. Of course, everything depends on the type of food you are cooking.

Let's take a quick look at temperature basics:

- **High heat:** This will cook your meals fast with a risk of burning if you're not careful. Think of this temperature as a frying pan or steamer.
- **Medium heat:** Slow and easy. It is a good temperature for eggs, toasting bread, etc. Think of this temperature as your oven. Medium to medium high is a good temperature to use the basting cover to melt cheese, steam vegetables, etc.
- **Low heat:** Think of this as the temperature of your charcoal grill. It will take longer to cook.

The Griddle Recipe Handbook

Best Temperature for a Variety of Food Types:

- **Low Heat:**
    - Fatty meats
- **Medium Heat:**
    - Seafood
    - Hamburgers
    - Toasting bread
    - Eggs
    - Pancakes
- **High Heat:**
    - Lean meats
    - Anything you want to sear and fast

Most of the recipes in the book use medium and medium-high heat. While several do use high heat to cook.

Best cook time for steaks:

The cook time for steaks depends on how you like your steak. Steaks can be enjoyed in any number of ways. The most popular include:

- Medium-rare: 3 to 5 minutes
- Medium: 5 to 7 minutes
- Medium-well: 8 to 10 minutes
- Well: 10 to 12 minutes
- Burnt: This is when you forgot about your steak. ▫

But no matter how you like your steak, remember to let your steak "settle" for about 5 minutes after you remove it from your griddle. Now let's turn our attention to some of the tools need to make these great tasting recipes in this recipe book.

The Griddle Recipe Handbook

Griddle Tools

Basting Covers

Several of the recipes in this book use a basting cover or basting dome. It is used to steam vegetables, melt cheese and more. They also help prevent grease splatters.

Covers are very versatile and are must-have for any griddle master. There are a few different options to choose from. You can purchase stainless steel basting covers or disposable aluminum covers. The stainless steel covers are more expensive and dishwasher safe, while the aluminum covers ones are less expensive and disposable.

The aluminum covers can also be used as a mixture pan when you use your flat top, too. It is a good idea to have at least a few covers handy while using your griddle. I have a few of the stainless covers and several of the aluminum covers, too.

If you notice, the aluminum ones are simply turkey basting pans. They are very inexpensive. A number of the recipes in this book, utilize the aluminum basting pans.

A popular griddling hack is to simply add a cabinet handle to the top and make your own large basting cover.

The Griddle Recipe Handbook

Cast Iron Grill Press

Weighted grill presses help to keep bacon, ham or other meats from curling. In addition, they help to keep your food healthy. When you place a grill press on a hamburger or a sausage, it presses out excess fat.

In addition, they also help to hold the heat for sandwiches. For steaks, the weighted press helps to distribute heat evenly.

In addition, some grill presses have raised strips to place grill marks on the food. While you don't need one to make great recipes, they are a must have for many griddle masters.

Cooling Racks

Cooling racks can be placed directly on the flat top surface or on a table. This allows the air to circulate on all sides of the food. They are very convenient to have. They are available in several different sizes.

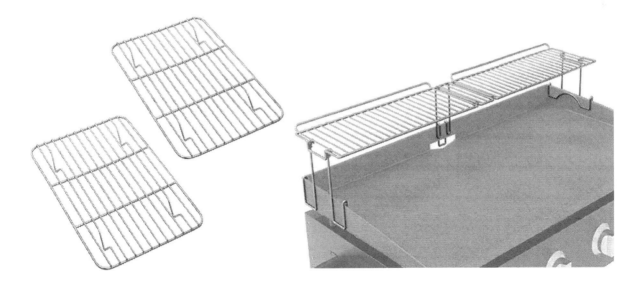

The Griddle Recipe Handbook

Spatulas, Egg Rings, Scrapers and More...

After a few short weeks of owning your griddle, you'll probably find yourself cooking breakfast, lunch and dinner as often as you can on it. Spatulas, egg rings and scrapers all make owning a flat top more enjoyable. All of recipes in this book use either spatulas, tongs or other griddling tools.

Let's get started...

The Griddle Recipe Handbook

Appetizers

Mozzarella Sticks Recipe

What You'll Need:

- 1 large egg
- ½ -1 lb. mozzarella block (or use pre-packed ones which are already cut and shaped like tiny hotdogs)
- ½ cup flour
- Salt and pepper to taste
- ½-1 cup panko breadcrumbs or you may also use plain breadcrumbs

Let's Fry Up Some Gooey Mozzarella!

1. Get everything you'll need to make the mozzarella sticks.

2. Cut up the mozzarella block into finger size pieces and season the flour with salt and pepper. Seasoning the flour adds a layer of flavor and makes your mozzarella sticks extra special!

3. Roll the mozzarella pieces in the flour, making sure the pieces are well covered. Shake off extra flour.

4. Beat the egg and season it with salt and pepper. Do the same for the breadcrumbs. Now dip the floured mozzarella pieces in the egg and then coat with breadcrumbs.

5. Do the same for all the mozzarella pieces. At this stage, you can wrap this in plastic wrap and freeze for up to a month if you are planning on having it later.

6. Preheat griddle to medium. Oil lightly. Place mozzarella sticks on flat top. Cover with basting cover. Turn once. Cook until soft.

7. Place in paper towel to soak up the excess oil and serve with your favorite marinara sauce recipe! Enjoy!

Using Frozen Mozzarella Cheese Sticks:
Another option is to use frozen cheese sticks. Simply follow the heating instructions above for great tasting cheese sticks.

The Griddle Recipe Handbook

Pesto Sauce with Rice Crackers Recipe

This is a great tasting sauce and pairs any number of food including round rice crackers, bruschetta, to dip pizza crust and more.

What You'll Need:

- Basil Leaves
- Parmesan Cheese
- Olive Oil – 5 tbsp
- Sunflower seeds – 100gms
- Walnuts – 100gms
- Garlic – 5 big pod or minced garlic 5 tablespoons
- Salt & Pepper to Taste

Let's Griddle!

1. Wash the basil leaves properly and then add them to the food processor. Then add 5 big pods of garlic or minced garlic, the walnuts and sunflower seeds. Grate the parmesan cheese into the food processor. Add salt and pepper according to taste.

2. Then finely blend them together to form a smooth paste.

3. Once this is done transfer the pesto sauce into a small container and add olive oil to it. To boost the shelf life of the pesto sauce in the fridge, make sure that it is completely covered with olive oil before sealing the container.

4. Then serve it with crackers at a party or you can also use it as a spread for breads. It not only is healthy but tastes exceptionally well.

5. Preheat griddle to medium. Oil lightly. Place round rice crackers until crispy on one side. Remove, cover with pesto spread and serve.

The Griddle Recipe Handbook

Super Stuffed Potato Skins

What You'll Need:

- 6 baking potatoes
- 1 c. shredded extra-sharp cheddar cheese
- 1 c. sour cream
- ¼ cup butter, melted
- 1 tsp. salt
- ½ tsp. pepper
- ¼ c. bacon bits
- 3 scallions, finely chopped
- ¼ c. sweet red pepper, finely chopped
- Paprika for garnish

Let's Griddle!

1. Scrub and pierce potatoes with a fork. Place potatoes in microwave for 6 to 7 minutes. Let cool.

2. Cut potatoes in half-length wise.

3. Scoop out most of the flesh and put it in a bowl leaving the skins. Brush the potatoes with butter

4. Add sour cream, cheddar cheese, bacon bits, scallions, red pepper, salt and pepper to the potatoes and mash to desired consistency.

5. Divide potato mixture evenly and return to skins.

6. Sprinkle with paprika and place on flat top skin side up. Griddle for 5 minutes, turn and cook for 4 minutes. Remove and top off with additional bacon and additional sour cream.

The Griddle Recipe Handbook

Super Cheesy and Easy Potato Wedges

What You'll Need:

- 6 baking potatoes
- 1 c. shredded extra-sharp cheddar cheese
- 1 c. sour cream
- ¼ cup butter, melted
- 4 strips of cooked bacon
- 3 scallions, finely chopped
- Rosemary, salt and pepper for garnish

Let's Griddle!

1. Scrub potatoes. Cut each potato lengthwise into 8 wedges; brush with oil. Sprinkle with rosemary, salt and pepper.

2. Prepare griddle for medium. Lightly oil.

3. Griddle 10 to 15 minutes or until potatoes are tender and browned, turning when needed. Cover with basting cover. Add a little water to the surface before you cover. This will help to "steam" the wedges.

4. Add cheese, remove once melted. Top off with bacon, sour cream and scallions.

The Griddle Recipe Handbook

Cheese and Bacon Stuffed Mini Sweet Peppers

What You'll Need:

- 1 bag mini sweet peppers in assorted colors
- 6 oz. goat cheese
- 6 oz. ricotta cheese
- 3 T. fresh thyme leaves, stems removed
- 4 strips thick-cut bacon, cooked and crumbled
- salt and pepper, to taste
- 1 oz. hard Parmesan cheese, freshly grated

Let's Griddle!

1. Wash peppers and pat dry. Cut each pepper in half lengthwise, leaving the stem intact. Remove seeds and membranes from each pepper half and discard. Set aside.

2. In a small bowl, combine goat cheese, ricotta cheese, thyme leaves and bacon and sprinkle with some salt and pepper. Combine ingredients thoroughly. With a small spoon, fill each pepper half with the cheese and bacon mixture and arrange on a rimmed baking sheet covered with parchment paper. Top each stuffed pepper half with grated Parmesan cheese

3. Prepare griddle for medium heat. Lightly oil. Place on griddle. Cover with basting cover. Add a little water to the surface before you cover.

4. Cook for approximately 5 minutes or until the cheese begins to brown and peppers start to blister. Remove and place on a serving plate. Serve immediately.

The Griddle Recipe Handbook

Stuffed Bell Peppers with Cheese and Homemade Crotons

What You'll Need:

- 4 bell peppers in assorted colors
- 6 oz. goat cheese
- 12 oz. gouda cheese
- 12 oz. jalapeno Havarti cheese
- Salt and pepper, to taste
- 4 slices of sour dough bread, but any white bread will do
- ¼ cup olive oil

Let's Griddle!

To Make Crotons

1. Lightly brush each side of bread with olive oil. Cut bread slices into small ¼ inch cubes. Add cubes to bread bowl. Add desired salt and pepper and toss gently.

2. Prepare griddle to medium. Place bread cubes on flat top until slightly brown and crispy. Remove and place on plate.

To Make Stuffed Peppers

1. Cut top off peppers and remove seeds.

2. Mix cheeses to together.

3. Place the crotons on the bottom of each pepper. Add cheese mixture inside each pepper.

4. Prepare griddle for medium heat. Lightly oil. Place peppers on griddle. Cover with basting cover. Add a little water to the surface before you cover.

5. Cook for approximately 7 to 10 minutes or until the cheese begins to brown and peppers start to blister. Remove and place on a serving plate. Serve immediately.

Recipe #2: Stuffed Bell Peppers with Cheese, Hamburger and Rice.

Another option is to add hamburger and onions to the peppers. Simply cook hamburger on your griddle. Mix with cooked rice. Replace the crotons with the cooked hamburger and rice, add the cheese mixture and cooked as mentioned above.

The Griddle Recipe Handbook

Bacon Jalapeño Cheese Ball Appetizer

What You'll Need:

- ✓ 8 thick-cut slices of bacon
- ✓ ½ large jalapeño pepper, finely minced, divided
- ✓ 8 oz. cream cheese, room temperature
- ✓ ½ c. Mexican-blend cheese, finely shredded
- ✓ ½ t. smoked paprika
- ✓ ½ t. Mexican oregano
- ✓ ½ t. chipotle powder
- ✓ ½ t. garlic powder
- ✓ Sea salt and black pepper, to taste
- ✓ To Serve: Vegetables, of choice or crackers

Let's Griddle!

1. Prepare griddle for medium heat. Lightly oil. Cook bacon until crispy. Remove and place on plate. Use paper towel to soak up any excess bacon grease.

2. Crush with hand into small pieces. Transfer bacon crumbs to a large bowl, along with half the jalapeño pepper, and stir to combine. Set aside.

3. Combine the remaining jalapeño pepper, cream cheese, Mexican cheese, smoked paprika, Mexican oregano, chipotle powder, and garlic powder in a large bowl. Season with salt and black pepper, to taste, and stir vigorously to combine.

4. Shape the cheese mixture into a ball with your hands and transfer to a serving plate. Place in the refrigerator to firm up a bit, approximately 5-10 minutes.

5. Remove cheese ball from refrigerator and gently roll in the bacon jalapeño mixture until thoroughly coated. Return to serving dish and serve immediately with sliced vegetables and/or gluten-free crackers. Enjoy!

6. Serve with bruschetta, crackers, etc.

The Griddle Recipe Handbook

Bacon-Wrapped Water Chestnuts with Spicy Mustard Dip

What You'll Need:

- 8 strips center-cut bacon
- 1/3 c. gluten-free soy sauce
- 3 T. honey, preferably local
- 2 8-oz. can water chestnuts, rinsed and drained
- ¾ c. Greek yogurt
- 2½ T. Dijon mustard
- 1 T. hot sauce
- ¼ t. cayenne pepper
- 2 T. fresh parsley, roughly chopped
- Sea salt and black pepper, to taste

Let's Griddle!

1. Cut bacon strips in half lengthwise, then cut each thin strip into 3 equal sections for a total of 48 pieces. Set aside.

2. Mix soy sauce and honey in a medium mixing bowl. Add water chestnuts and turn to coat. Marinate at room temperature for approximately 30 minutes, turning water chestnuts 2-3 times during that time.

3. Preheat oven to 400°F and place a metal rack inside a large, rimmed baking sheet. Spray rack with non-stick cooking spray and set aside.

4. Drain water chestnuts, but reserve the marinade. Wrap each water chestnut with a piece of bacon, then repeat with a second strip on the opposite side. Secure both pieces of bacon with a toothpick and place on baking rack.

5. Repeat with remaining water chestnuts. Each appetizer with reserved marinade on all sides. Prepare griddle for medium heat. Lightly oil. Place on griddle. Cover with basting cover. Check every few minutes to ensure bacon isn't burning. Turn as needed.

6. While the water chestnuts are roasting, combine Greek yogurt, Dijon mustard, hot sauce, cayenne pepper, and parsley in a small bowl. Season salt and black pepper, to taste. Cover and place in the refrigerator until ready to serve.

7. When finished, remove the bacon-wrapped water chestnuts from the griddle and serve immediately with the spicy mustard sauce for dipping. Enjoy!

The Griddle Recipe Handbook

Bruschetta with Mushrooms & Herbed Cheese

What You'll Need:

- 5 T. unsalted butter, divided
- 2 T. olive oil
- 1/2 medium shallot, finely minced
- 2 cloves garlic, peeled finely minced
- 1 c. white mushrooms, cleaned and chopped
- 1 c. baby Portobello mushrooms, cleaned and chopped
- 2 t. fresh thyme leaves, stems removed
- 1 1.2 T. fresh rosemary, stems removed and leaves finely chopped
- 1/4 c. brandy or peach juice
- salt and pepper to taste
- 4 oz. goat cheese, room temperature
  4 oz. ricotta cheese
  2 t. fresh thyme leaves, stems removed
- 2 t. fresh rosemary, stems removed and leaves finely chopped
- 2 small 6" Ciabatta loafs, cut in half lengthwise, then cut into 2-3" sections

Let's Griddle!

1. Prepare griddle for medium heat. Lightly oil.

2. In small pan from your kitchen placed on your flat top melt 1 T. butter. Add oil and shallots and sauté 2 minutes. Add garlic and sauté 2 more minutes. Add mushrooms and sauté approximately 8-10 minutes or until mushrooms release juices. Add thyme and rosemary and sauté 2 additional minutes.

3. Stir in brandy or peach juice and simmer until reduced by half. Remove from heat and whisk in 2 T. butter. If desired, season to taste with salt and pepper.

4. In a separate bowl, mix goat cheese with ricotta cheese and fresh herbs until well combined.

5. Butter bread slices with remaining 2 T. butter and place on griddle. Toast until golden brown. Then, spread with herbed goat cheese mixture and top with mushrooms. Serve immediately.

The Griddle Recipe Handbook

Blackened Broccoli Side Dish

What You'll Need:

- ✓ 2 heads fresh broccoli, washed and florets removed (stalks and stems reserved for another use) or
- ✓ 2 12 oz. bags of frozen broccoli florets
- ✓ 2 T. water
- ✓ 3 cloves garlic, peeled and finely minced
- ✓ 2 T. olive oil, divided
- ✓ 1 t. crushed red pepper flakes (optional)
- ✓ 2 T. unsalted butter, divided
- ✓ 2 T. sesame oil
- ✓ salt and pepper, to taste

Let's Griddle!

1. Prepare griddle for medium heat. Lightly oil. Add one half of the chopped garlic to griddle. Add ½ teaspoon crushed red pepper flakes (if desired) and one tablespoon of butter.

2. Cook garlic over medium heat for approximately 1-2 minutes, stirring constantly. Increase heat to medium-high and add ½ broccoli florets. Stir broccoli constantly while searing the florets.

3. Once blackened, remove the broccoli from the griddle and place in a large glass bowl. Cover and keep warm.

4. Repeat process with remaining garlic, olive oil, red pepper, butter and broccoli.

5. When second batch of broccoli is finished, add it to the bowl with the original batch. Drizzle with sesame oil and toss to coat. Season with salt and pepper, to taste. Serve immediately.

The Griddle Recipe Handbook

Portobello and Sage-Stuffed Acorn Squash

What You'll Need:

- ✓ 3 acorn squash, cut in half and seeds removed
- ✓ 3 T. extra virgin olive oil, divided
- ✓ 3-4 cloves garlic, finely minced
- ✓ 4 oz. pancetta, diced
- ✓ 1½ lbs. Portobello mushrooms, roughly chopped
- ✓ ½ medium yellow onion, thinly sliced
- ✓ 1 c. green lentils, cooked
- ✓ 1 1/2 T. fresh sage, finely chopped
- ✓ ¼ c. dry red wine
- ✓ 1/3 c. dates, roughly chopped
- ✓ ¼ c. walnuts, chopped
- ✓ ¼ c. Parmesan cheese, freshly grated
- ✓ Sea salt and pepper to taste

Let's Griddle!

1. Prepare griddle for medium heat. Lightly oil. Place on griddle. Place the acorn squash halves cut side up in prepared baking dish and brush cut edges with one tablespoon olive oil. Season with salt and black pepper, to taste. Place on griddle top with cut side down. Cover with basting cover. Add a little water to the surface before you cover. Check every 5 minutes until fork tender. Continue to add water with each check.

2. Add chopped mushrooms, garlic and cook, stirring occasionally, until they start to brown, approximately 4-5 minutes. Add sliced onions and continue cooking, stirring once or twice, for another 3-4 minutes.

3. Place aluminum roasting pan on your flat top. Stir in mushrooms, garlic, onions, green lentils, fresh sage, and red wine into pan. Cook, stirring occasionally, until mixture thickens, approximately 8-10 minutes. Remove from heat and stir in the chopped dates and toasted walnuts. Season with salt and black pepper, to taste. Set aside.

4. When ready, remove cooked squash cool slightly before filling each half with the Portobello mushroom mixture. Sprinkle each half with some freshly grated Parmesan cheese.

5. Return stuffed squash griddle and cover for another 5-10 minutes, or until heated through and the cheese starts to melt. Remove from oven and serve.

The Griddle Recipe Handbook

Breakfast Recipes

Hard Boiled Eggs

What You'll Need:

- ✓ Fresh eggs in any number you want
- ✓ Basting dome

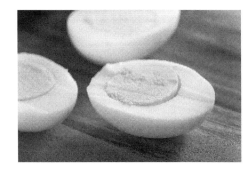

Let's Make a Hard-Boiled Egg!

1. Preheat your griddle to medium.

2. Total griddle time is 12 minutes.

3. Place eggs on flat top and cover with bashing dome. Add a little water to the surface before you cover.

4. Set an alarm for every 3 minutes. Uncover, rotate egg and add water under the cover each time the timer goes off.

5. Remove from heat and transfer to a plate to let cool.

The Griddle Recipe Handbook

Inside Out Scotch Eggs

What You'll Need:

- ✓ Breakfast sausage meat
- ✓ 4 large hard-boiled eggs made on your flat top. See hard-boiled eggs recipe in this book.
- ✓ 1 teaspoon of black pepper
- ✓ 1 teaspoon of salt

Let's Griddle!

1. Place the black pepper, salt and sausage meat into the mixing bowl and stir well with the wooden spoon until all the ingredients are combined.

2. Prepare griddle for medium heat. Lightly oil. Cook sausage until done. Remove sausage and place on plate.

3. Cut hard-boiled egg in half and place on sausage. Serve and enjoy.

Traditional Scotch Eggs

The traditional scotch egg recipe is when the sausage is wrapped around the outside of a hard-boiled egg.

Let's Griddle!

1. Using the uncooked sausage, simply wrap a hard-boiled egg with the uncooked breakfast sausage.

2. Prepare griddle for medium heat. Lightly oil. Place on griddle. Place sausage covered hard-boiled eggs on flat top. Cover with basting cover. Add a little water to the surface before you cover Total cook time is 4 to 5 minutes.

3. Roll every few minutes until done. Check sausage to ensure it is thoroughly cooked. Remove from heat, let cool and serve.

The Griddle Recipe Handbook

Bell Pepper & Onion Omelet

What You'll Need:

- 8 large eggs
- 2 cups of milk
- 1 chopped medium bell pepper
- 1 chopped medium onion
- 1 tablespoon of butter
- 1 teaspoon of black pepper
- 1 teaspoon of salt
- ½ cup of shredded cheddar cheese

Let's Griddle!

1. Prepare griddle for medium heat. Lightly oil.

2. Add the chopped bell pepper and onion pieces to the griddle for 2 to 3 minutes.

3. While the bell peppers and onions are cooking, add the black pepper, eggs, grated cheddar cheese, milk and salt to the mixing bowl and mix with the wooden spoon.

4. After the bell peppers and onion done, pour the ingredients from the mixing bowl into the griddle and fry until the omelet starts to thicken (this usually takes about 2 minutes).

5. Once the top of the omelet starts to turn brown, remove, divide the omelet into four sections with the spatula, put a section on each of the four plates, serve and enjoy.

The Griddle Recipe Handbook

Chicken & Ham Fried Eggs

What You'll Need:

- ✓ 8 large eggs
- ✓ 1 cup of chopped cooked chicken
- ✓ 1 cup of chopped cooked ham
- ✓ 1 tablespoon of butter
- ✓ 1 teaspoon of black pepper
- ✓ 1 teaspoon of salt

Let's Griddle!

1. Prepare griddle for medium-high heat. Lightly oil.

2. Add the chopped chicken and ham pieces until slightly brown and crispy.

3. Use the spatula to ensure that the chicken and ham are evenly distributed and then add the eggs.

4. Fry the eggs until they have turned from clear to white (this usually takes 2 minutes), then remove.

5. Divide the chicken and ham fried eggs into four portions using the spatula, put a section on each of the four plates, serve and enjoy.

The Griddle Recipe Handbook

Chopped Tomatoes & Scrambled Eggs

What You'll Need:

- 8 large eggs
- 4 chopped large tomatoes
- 2 cups of milk
- 1 teaspoon of black pepper
- 1 teaspoon of dried oregano
- 1 teaspoon of dried thyme
- 1 teaspoon of salt

Let's Griddle!

1. Prepare griddle for medium-high heat. Lightly oil.

2. Mix together black pepper, eggs, milk and salt and add to the griddle.

3. Once the eggs have set and become fluffy, remove from the heat. Place in glass bowl.

4. Add the chopped tomatoes, dried oregano and dried thyme and stir well with the wooden spoon.

5. Divide the chopped tomatoes and scrambled eggs mixture into four portions using the spatula, put a section on each of the four plates, serve and enjoy.

The Griddle Recipe Handbook

Sausage, Egg and Cheese Sandwich

What You'll Need:

- ✓ Breakfast sausage meat
- ✓ 1 bagel
- ✓ 1 egg
- ✓ Pepper, to taste
- ✓ Cheddar cheese, sliced

Let's Griddle!

1. Prepare griddle for medium heat. Lightly oil.

2. Cook sausage and egg as usual. Cook egg sunny side up.

3. Place on flat side of each bagel on the griddle. Cook until slightly brown and crispy.

4. Layer cheese, sausage and egg on bottom half of bagel. Place top of bagel to make the sandwich. Remove to unheated portion of the griddle. Cover with basting cover for 1 minute to allow cheese to melt. Remove and enjoy.

Open-Faced Egg Sandwich

What You'll Need:

- ✓ Slice of sour dough bread
- ✓ 2 eggs
- ✓ Deli ham or breakfast sausage
- ✓ Cheddar cheese, sliced

Let's Griddle!

1. Prepare griddle for medium heat. Lightly oil.

2. Cook sausage/ham and egg as usual. Cook egg sunny side up. Place bread slice on griddle until one side is crispy.

3. Layer cheese, sausage/ham and egg

4. Remove to unheated portion of the griddle. Cover with basting cover for 1 minute to allow cheese to melt. Remove and enjoy.

The Griddle Recipe Handbook

Pumpkin Spice Pancakes

What You'll Need:

- 6 large eggs
- 2/3 c. pure pumpkin puree
- 2 T. honey
- ½ c. almond flour
- ½ c. coconut flour
- 1½ t. baking powder
- 1 T. pumpkin pie spice
- 1/8 t. salt
- 3 T. coconut oil, divided
- Optional: 1 banana, sliced thin; 1/3 c. pecans

Let's Griddle!

1. In a large mixing bowl, whisk the eggs, pumpkin puree, and honey until thoroughly combined.

2. In a separate bowl, combine the almond flour, coconut flour, baking powder, pumpkin pie spice, and salt.

3. Add the dry ingredients to the bowl with the egg mixture and gently fold the two together until blended.

4. Prepare griddle to medium heat. Once hot, spoon 2-3 tablespoons per pancake and cook for 3 minutes on the first side, then flip and cook for another 2-3 minutes on the other side. Repeat this process with remaining coconut oil and pancake batter.

5. To serve, stack 2-3 pancakes per serving and top with sliced bananas, chopped pecans, and a drizzle of maple syrup, if desired. Enjoy!

The Griddle Recipe Handbook

Flourless Protein Pancakes

What You'll Need:

- 1 Medium ripe banana
- 1/3 cup instant oats
- 2 eggs
- A nob of butter
- Honey or agave syrup for garnish

Let's Griddle!

1. Start by mashing the banana until no more big bits are left.

2. Add the eggs. Add the oats. Mix everything until well combined.

3. Cook a quarter cup to a third of a cup of the mixture on a medium heated griddle with a bit of butter or oil.

4. Turn-over and cook the other side until done.

5. Take off the heat and transfer to a plate.

6. Drizzle with a 1-2 teaspoons of agave syrup and add a bit of butter of desired.

7. Makes 4 pancakes. Serves 2 for snacks or 1 for a very filling breakfast!

The Griddle Recipe Handbook

Coconut Flour Pancakes

For avoid lumps, sift the coconut flour before adding to the batter. If you don't have a sifter, pour flour into a fine-mesh sieve and gently shake over the bowl.

What You'll Need:

- 1 large egg
- 2 egg whites
- 1½ T. pure maple syrup
- 3 T. very mild olive oil
- 1 t. pure vanilla extract
- ½ c. coconut milk
- 1/3 c. coconut flour, sifted
- ½ t. baking powder
- Pinch salt
- 3 T. coconut oil, divided
- 1 large banana, sliced
- 2 c. fresh raspberries
- Real maple syrup, for serving

Let's Griddle!

1. In a large mixing bowl, whisk the egg, egg whites, maple syrup, olive oil, and vanilla extract until smooth. Pour in the coconut milk and whisk to combine.

2. Add the sifted coconut flour, baking powder, and a small pinch of salt. Gently fold in the dry ingredients without overworking the batter.

3. Melt about a teaspoon of coconut oil on prepared medium heated griddle and pour 2-3 tablespoons of batter per pancake. Cook until the pancakes are set and the edges turn a deeper golden color, around 1-2 minutes.

4. Flip and cook the remaining side another 1-2 minutes, or until golden brown. Remove from heat and repeat this process with the remaining batter.

5. To serve, stack several pancakes and top with sliced banana, raspberries, and drizzle with real maple syrup, if desired. Enjoy!

The Griddle Recipe Handbook

Easy Parmesan Breakfast Potatoes

Let's Griddle!

- ✓ 3 large baking potatoes, diced
- ✓ 1 T. water
- ✓ 1 T. extra virgin olive oil
- ✓ 1 medium red bell pepper, diced
- ✓ ½ medium red onion, diced
- ✓ ½ t. garlic powder
- ✓ ½ t. dried parsley
- ✓ ½ t. dried rosemary
- ✓ ½ t. smoked paprika
- ✓ Sea salt and black pepper, to taste
- ✓ ¼ c. Parmesan cheese, freshly grated

Let's Griddle!

1. Cut potatoes in small cubes.

2. Prepare griddle for medium heat. Lightly oil. Place potatoes, onions, peppers on griddle. Cover with basting cover. Add a little water to the surface before you cover. Cook until golden brown and slightly crispy. Don't overcook. Sprinkle with garlic powder, parsley, rosemary, and smoked paprika. Season with salt and black pepper, to taste, and stir to combine.

3. Remove from heat and sprinkle freshly grated Parmesan cheese on top of the warm potatoes. Cover just until the cheese melts and serve immediately. Enjoy!

The Griddle Recipe Handbook

Lunch – Wraps, Sandwiches and More Recipes

Chicken BBQ Wrap Recipe

What You'll Need:

- ½ cup of shredded chicken meat (from chicken barbecue or perhaps roasted chicken)
- 1 10-12-inch flour tortilla
- 1 small red onion, chopped thinly
- 2 small tomatoes or 1 big one, sliced thinly as well
- 1/3-1/2 cup ranch dressing or your favorite creamy and tart dressing
- 2 cups of assorted lettuce leaves or your favorite greens

Let's Griddle!

1. Make sure you've got all the ingredients that you need.

2. Prepare the ingredients, chop what need to be chopped, shred what needs to be shredded.

3. Preheat to medium-low. Prepare with oil.

4. Place your tortilla on the griddle until slightly brown. Allow to cool.

5. It's time to wrap things up! Just layer the tomatoes, onions, and lettuce on top on the tortilla and top it off with 2-3 tablespoons of the ranch dressing.

6. Roll it tightly and place back on griddle and roll back and forth for a few minutes to slightly heat.

7. Remove and slice up or serve as 1 whole piece as a complete meal!

The Griddle Recipe Handbook

Deluxe Griddled Chicken Sandwiches

What You'll Need:

- 1 lb. breast of chicken, cut into strips
- 1 md green pepper thin, sliced
- 1 md red bell pepper thin, sliced
- 1 md onion thinly, sliced
- 4 oz Monterey jack (or mozzarella) cheese, sliced
- 1/4 t garlic powder
- 1 T taco seasoning
- 1 salt and pepper, to taste
- 4 buns, your choice
- 1/2 t basil, dried

Let's Griddle!

1. Sauté chicken breast, sprinkle with garlic powder, salt, pepper and taco seasoning.

2. Prepare griddle for medium heat. Lightly oil. Add peppers, onion, sauté till tender, and chicken is no longer pink.

3. Butter outside of sliced buns sprinkle with basil if desired, place on griddle and crisp bun. Remove bun and put chicken mixture in bun.

4. Top each sandwich with grated cheese. Place back on griddle and cover until cheese bubbles and begins browning. Serve with cucumber spears.

The Griddle Recipe Handbook

Hawaiian Ham & Pineapple Grilled Cheese Sandwich Recipe

What You Will Need:

- ✓ Half a baguette cut lengthwise
- ✓ 2/3 to 1 cup of your favorite cheese (in this recipe we use mozzarella and mild cheddar mix)
- ✓ 4 ounces of ham, chopped into strips
- ✓ One medium sized red onion, cut into rings
- ✓ Half a cup of pineapple chunks

Time to Create a Mean Cheese Sandwich!

1. Gather all your ingredients. It is best to have everything prepared at the start for faster cooking time later.

2. Preheat griddle to medium-high. Oil lightly. Place the ham on the griddle until slightly crisp. Set aside.

3. Increase the heat to medium high, place the pineapples and onions until they develop some color or caramelizes a bit.

4. On your bread, add half of the cheese, spreading them out.

5. Place the ham and onions over the bread and cheese.

6. Add in the pineapples and the remaining cheese.

7. Move to a non-heated heat zone on your flat top and place under melting dome or cover under aluminum foil until the cheese has fully melted.

8. Here are the lovely halves of your sandwich! If you like, you can serve it this way as an open-faced sandwich, but its double the goodness when you slap them together to create a grilled cheese sandwich overload.

9. One serving is half of the done sandwich.

Or enjoy it as mini sandwiches by cutting it into 4. You may add in some mustard or barbecue sauce, but it's really not needed, and the juicy pineapple and the ham makes for a perfect combination together with then onion and creamy cheese.

The Griddle Recipe Handbook

Amazing Grilled Cheese Crab and Lobster Sandwich

What You Will Need:

- 4 slices of bread or bun, sourdough or bread of your choice
- ½ cup Gruyere cheese, shredded
- ½ cup Monterey Jack cheese, shredded
- ¼ cup white cheddar cheese, shredded
- 8 oz. of imitation lobster
- 8 oz. of imitation crab

Time to Create an Amazing Grilled Cheese Crab and Lobster Sandwich!

1. Combine Gruyere, Monterey Jack and white cheddar together in a bowl. Cut the lobster and crab into bite size chunks and mix in separate bowl.

2. Preheat griddle to medium-low. Lightly oil your griddle. Place bread on griddle and toast until golden brown. Place large handful of mixed cheese on the flat top. The cheese will begin to melt. Place mixed lobster and crab chunks on the griddle until slightly crispy.

3. Place the non-toasted side of bread onto the melted cheese. Turn over so the melted cheese will be facing up. Immediately, place the crab and lobster combine into the bread slices, combination slice to make your sandwich and enjoy.

4. Serve immediately.

The Griddle Recipe Handbook

Honey Cheddar Sourdough Grilled Cheese Recipe

What You'll Need:

- Sliced sourdough bread
- Honey
- Cheddar slices (use sharp cheddar for best contrast of flavors)
- Butter
- Any easy melting cheese of your choice

Let's Make Some Awesome Griddled Cheese!

1. Preheat your griddle to medium-high as you prepare all your ingredients.

2. Lay down some cheddar slices on a slice of bread.

3. Drizzle in some honey, and then add the easy-melt cheese.

4. Add another slice of bread to make a sandwich and spread some butter over it.

5. Place on a griddle and 'cook' each side until well browned and cheese is melted. Place under melting dome or cover under aluminum foil.

6. Slice diagonally and serve up!

7. Make as much as you want or make an entire batch for everyone! You can also make this ahead of time and freeze until you are ready to heat up your pan or grill. Enjoy!

The Griddle Recipe Handbook

Spinach & Soy Sauce Turkey Wraps

What You'll Need:

- 16 oz. of turkey (sliced into four separate 4 oz. pieces)
- 16 large spinach leaves
- 4 tablespoons of soy sauce
- 2 tablespoon of extra virgin olive oil
- 1 teaspoon of black pepper
- 1 teaspoon of salt

Let's Griddle!

1. Place the black pepper, salt and soy sauce into the mixing bowl and mix them together to form a marinade.
2. Once the marinade ingredients are fully mixed, add the sliced turkey to the mixing bowl and fully coat all the slices in marinade.
3. Once the sliced turkey is fully coated in the marinade, wrap the mixing bowl with plastic food wrap and refrigerate for a minimum of 4 hours to allow the marinade to fully soak into the sliced turkey.
4. After 4 hours, remove the mixing bowl from the refrigerator and pre-heat the griddle to a medium-high heat.
5. Grill the sliced turkey for 5 minutes on each side then remove it from the flat top and turn off the heat.
6. Wrap each of the four portions of turkey in four spinach leaves.
7. If you are eating the wraps there and then, place one onto each of the four plates, serve and enjoy. Alternatively, if you are eating the wraps later, place a wrap into each of the four sealable containers and then put them in the refrigerator until you are ready to eat.

The Griddle Recipe Handbook

Chunky Chicken Salad Lettuce Wraps

TIP: Boston Bibb lettuce is another excellent lettuce variety for this recipe because it has attractive, naturally bowl-shaped leaves.

What You'll Need:

Dressing:

- 1 T. avocado mayonnaise
- 2 T. Greek yogurt
- 2 t. Dijon mustard
- 1 T. red wine vinegar
- ½ t. garlic powder
- 2 t. dried oregano
- Sea salt and black pepper, to taste

Chicken Salad:

- 12 oz. rotisserie or griddle cooked chicken breast, chuck into equal size cubes
- 3 large stalks celery, chopped
- 3/4 c. pecans, roughly chopped
- 15 red grapes, washed and cut in half
- 3 T. fresh parsley, washed, stems removed and finely chopped
- 2 green onions, finely sliced, green part only
- 4-6 large Romaine lettuce leaves
- Sea salt and black pepper, to taste
- Garnish (optional) chopped fresh parsley; Sliced green onions

Let's Griddle!

1. In a small glass bowl, combine avocado mayonnaise, Greek yogurt, Dijon mustard, red wine vinegar, garlic powder, and oregano. Stir to combine thoroughly. Season with salt and pepper, to taste. Set aside.

2. In a larger non-reactive bowl, combine chicken breast, celery, pecans, grapes, parsley, and green onion. Add dressing and gently stir to combine all ingredients thoroughly. Season with additional salt and pepper, if desired.

3. Cover and place in refrigerator for at least 30 minutes to overnight to allow the flavors to combine. To serve, divide the chicken salad between the Romaine lettuce leaves. Garnish with parsley and/or green onions, if desired, and serve immediately. Enjoy!

The Griddle Recipe Handbook

Taco-Stuffed Portobello Mushroom Caps

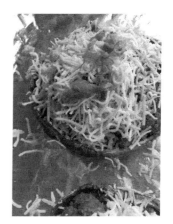

These delicious low-carb stuffed Portobello mushroom caps are really easy to make and deliver a ton of flavor. Taco Tuesday will never be the same!

Use your favorite taco seasoning.

What You'll Need:

- 3 T. extra virgin olive oil
- 6 large Portobello mushroom caps, stems and gills removed
- 1 lb. lean ground beef
- 2–3 T. taco seasoning – Use your favorite seasoning
- ½ c. water
- 10 oz. four cheese Mexican-blend, finely shredded, divided
  4 green onions, green part only, finely sliced
- ½ pint grape tomatoes, washed and cut in quarters
- 1 avocado, seed and skin removed, cut into small chunks

Let's Griddle!

1. With a pastry brush, brush olive oil on outside of each mushroom cap, and around the interior and edges. Set finished caps on plate and set aside.

2. Over medium-high heat, brown ground beef on flat top until no longer pink inside.

3. Add 2-3 T. taco seasoning mix and ½ cup water to flat top. Stir to distribute taco seasoning evenly. Cook on medium-high heat for 5-7 minutes or until excess water cooks down, stirring occasionally. Remove from heat and cool for a couple of minutes.

4. Divide the seasoned beef among the 6 mushroom caps. Add approximately 1 oz. of shredded Mexican cheese to each cap. Place back on flat top. Cover with basting cover. Add a little water to the surface before you cover. Cook for approximately 5 to 7 minutes, or until cheese is melted. Remove from heat and cool for a couple of minutes before serving.

5. To serve, top with chopped tomatoes, avocado, remaining cheese, and green onions. Enjoy!

The Griddle Recipe Handbook

The Griddle Recipe Handbook

Super Easy Tri-Color Griddled Carrots

What You'll Need:

- ✓ 1½ lbs. tri-color carrots, washed and patted dry
- ✓ 2 T. olive oil
- ✓ 2 t. kosher salt
- ✓ 3 T. fresh thyme, stems removed

Let's Griddle!

1. Prepare griddle for medium heat. Lightly oil.

2. Place carrots baking sheet and drizzle with olive oil. Gently toss with your hands to evenly coat carrots with the oil. Sprinkle with salt and fresh thyme leaves. Toss to combine.

3. Place on griddle. Cover with basting cover. Add a little water to the surface before you cover. Cook for approximately 5 to 7 minutes. Remove cover, turn to expose the bottom side. Add a little water to the surface before you cover. Cook another 5-10 minutes or until they start to brown.

4. Remove from oven and serve immediately. Enjoy!

The Griddle Recipe Handbook

Mediterranean-Inspired Stuffed Portobello Mushrooms

What You'll Need:

- ✓ 6 large Portobello mushroom caps, stems and gills removed
- ✓ 3 T. extra virgin olive oil
- ✓ 6 oz. fresh or shredded mozzarella cheese
- ✓ ½ pint grape tomatoes, washed, dried, and cut in half
- ✓ ½ c. fresh or bottled pesto
- ✓ Sea salt and black pepper, to taste
- ✓ Garnish (optional): Aged balsamic vinegar or glaze

Let's Griddle!

1. With a pastry brush, brush olive oil on outside of each mushroom cap, and around the interior and edges. Place oiled caps on plate and evenly divide the mozzarella cheese between them. Top each cap with grape tomatoes and drizzle with pesto. Sprinkle with salt and black pepper, to taste.

2. Prepare griddle for medium heat. Lightly oil. Place mushrooms. Cover with basting cover. Add a little water to the surface before you cover. Cook for approximately 5 to 7 minutes, or until cheese is melted. Remove from heat and drizzle with aged balsamic vinegar or a thicker glaze, if desired. Serve immediately. Enjoy!

The Griddle Recipe Handbook

Warm Turkey, Pesto and Provolone Sandwich

Pesto What You'll Need:

- 3 cups fresh basil leaves
- 3 cloves garlic
- ½ cup toasted pine nuts
- ½ cup high-quality extra virgin olive oil
- salt and pepper, to taste
- ½ cup hard cheese, like Parmigiano-Reggiano, finely grated

Sandwich What You'll Need:

- 2 crusty French rolls
- 2 T. butter, unsalted
- 5 T. pesto (recipe included)
- 6-8 oz. deli turkey breast, thin sliced
- 4 oz. Provolone cheese, sliced

Let's Griddle!

1. To prepare the pesto, combine basil, garlic and pine nuts in a food processor container. Pulse until coarsely ground. Slowly add the olive oil and blend until the mixture becomes smooth. Transfer to glass bowl and season with salt and pepper. Stir in grated cheese until thoroughly combined and use immediately.

2. Freeze unused portion in ice cube trays and top with additional olive oil. Use frozen pesto cubes in soups or stews for additional flavor, as needed.

3. Cut the French rolls in half lengthwise and butter the inside portion of both halves. Place buttered side down on griddle over medium heat. Press down on the outside of the roll to help to make crispy. When golden brown, remove from heat and spread a generous amount of pesto on the warm, grilled portion of each piece.

4. Quickly heat turkey on flat top until warm. Add turkey and Provolone cheese to each roll. The heat from the turkey and the grilled roll should melt the cheese. Or place under basting cover on an unheated zone to melt the cheese. Serve immediately.

The Griddle Recipe Handbook

Dessert and Snack Recipes

Fruits & Cream Tortillas

For an exceptional twist on fruit desserts, try this fruits and cream tortilla recipe. You may have this as a snack, as a dessert, or just to have something new and unique to indulge your sweet tooth. Imagine crisped up whole wheat tortilla smothered in fluffy whipped cream with a hidden brown sugar crunch and some tart berries. It's refreshing and indulgent at the same time.

What You Will Need:

- ✓ 1 10-12-inch whole wheat tortilla (you may use a regular one instead)
- ✓ 2-3 tablespoons brown sugar
- ✓ ½ cup whipping cream or 1-1/2 cup fully whipped cream
- ✓ ½ cup fresh or frozen raspberries (you may use strawberries too)
- ✓ ½ cup fresh or frozen blackberries (you may use blueberries too)
- ✓ 2 halves of canned peaches (or use fresh peaches)

Sweeten Up Some Tortilla!

1. Gather everything you need for the fruits and cream tortilla.
2. Preheat griddle to medium. Oil lightly.
3. Spread the brown sugar over the tortilla. Place under melting dome or place loose aluminum foil over the tortilla until slightly crisping the sugar.
4. Once the tortilla has been browned and has crisped up, set aside until cooled before the next step.
5. Whip up the cream or use store bought whipped cream.
6. Dollop the whipped cream over the tortilla a few minutes before serving.
7. Slice the peaches into thin wedges and arrange over the cream.
8. Add in the berries and serve like fruit pizza.
9. Best enjoyed with hot tea or coffee.

The Griddle Recipe Handbook

Coconut Balls – Cardamom

What You'll Need:

- ✓ Dry Coconut Powder
- ✓ Cardamom Power – 1 tbsp.
- ✓ Grated Coconut – 1 ½ coconut
- ✓ Clarified Butter (Ghee) – 2 tbsp.
- ✓ Condensed Milk – 2 tbsp.

Let's Griddle!

1. Prepare all the ingredients in advance.
2. Preheat griddle to medium-low. Add butter or oil.
3. Add the grated coconut to griddle top.
4. Cook it till it turns slightly golden brown.
5. Then add the condensed milk. I added 2 tbsp. of condensed milk into it. The choice is actually yours. If you like it sweet you can add more.
6. Spread out the coconut mixture to ensure an even cook.
7. Cook for 5 minutes. The coconut will cook better with the condensed milk in it. The coconut will absorb the condensed milk.
8. Add 1 tbsp. of Cardamom Powder into the mixture. Cook it till it becomes slightly more golden brown and then take it off the flat top and let it cool down.
9. Then in another plate add the dry coconut powder.
10. Apply some clarified butter on your palm and then take 2 spoons of the mixture into your palm.
11. Make a ball out of the mixture in your hand.
12. Once you have acquired the right shape put the cardamom coconut ball into the dry coconut powder and cover it up. This will secure the ball from falling apart.
13. There you go, simple Cardamom Coconut Balls are ready to be eaten. Enjoy!

The Griddle Recipe Handbook

Crispy Chocolate Covered Banana Treats Recipe

What You'll Need:

- ✓ Several bananas
- ✓ A block of sweetened chocolate or several Heresy's chocolate bars
- ✓ Several popsicle sticks
- ✓ Rainbow sprinkles

Let Griddle!

1. Peel the bananas.
2. Cut the bananas in half.
3. Stick the bananas on the popsicle sticks.
4. Prepare a heat zone to medium-high. Lightly oil and place banana on heated griddle for approximately 2 minutes. Continuously roll the banana to prevent burning yet allowing a slight caramelization. Remove and let cool.
5. Slice the chocolate bar or Hersey's chocolate bars into small pieces and in a roasting pan on griddle top.
6. Prepare your griddle to medium-low and melt to chocolate. Make sure to check the chocolate every minute to make sure that the chocolate will melt evenly and prevent it from burning.
7. Dip the banana on the melted chocolate. Be quick in doing this step since most of the melted chocolate tends to solidify in an instant. That would still vary on the type of chocolate bar you used. You have the option to cover it completely or leave the bottom part bare, it is all up to you.
8. Carefully sprinkle the rainbow sprinkles around the chocolate-covered banana. This is perfectly done when the chocolate is still in its liquid or semi-liquid state. Put the chocolate-covered bananas in the freezer for 30 minutes.
9. Finally done!

The Griddle Recipe Handbook

Rum Glazed Bananas – An Adult Treat

What You'll Need:

- ✓ 4 bananas
- ✓ 3 tablespoons rum
- ✓ 2 tablespoons honey
- ✓ 1 teaspoon ground cinnamon
- ✓ Whipped cream or vanilla ice cream
- ✓ ½ cup walnut, if desired

Let's Griddle!

1. In a bowl, combine rum, honey and cinnamon; set aside

2. Cut bananas in half longways. Remove peel.

3. Preheat griddle to medium. Oil lightly.

4. Place bananas on griddle, flat side down. Brush with rum mixture. Place under melting dome or cover under aluminum foil until tender. Pour excess rum mixture over bananas when removed.

5. Serve immediately.

The Griddle Recipe Handbook

Blueberries & Honey Roasted Almonds

Blueberries and honey roasted almonds are a brilliant alternative to candy. Not only are they virtually carb free but they're also 100% natural, packed full of health boosting nutrients and extremely filling.

What You'll Need:

- 2 tablespoons of butter
- 1 cup of blueberries
- 1 cup of almonds
- 1 tablespoon of honey

Let's Griddle!

1. Place the butter and honey on a medium heat griddle and heat it until the butter melts and the honey becomes runny.

2. Once the butter and honey are runny, add the almonds and stir until they are fully coated in the mixture.

3. Once the almonds are fully coated, reduce heat to low. Cover and for 15 to 18 minutes. Stirring frequently until golden brown.

4. Remove and let the honey roasted almonds cool for 1 hour.

5. After 1 hour, place four equal portions of honey roasted almonds into each of the four small plastic food bags, add four equal portions of blueberries to each of the small plastic food bags and then grab a bag whenever you need a portable snack.

The Griddle Recipe Handbook

Dark Chocolate Brazil Nuts

What You'll Need:

- ✓ 16 Brazil nuts
- ✓ 2 oz. dark chocolate (chopped into chunks)
- ✓ 2 tablespoons of extra virgin olive oil

Let's Griddle!

1. Prepare griddle for low heat. Lightly oil. Place Brazil nuts on flat top. Cover with basting cover. Add a little water to the surface before you cover. Cook for 15 to 18 minutes. Stirring frequently until golden brown.

2. Place the dark chocolate chunks into the microwaveable bowl, put the bowl in the microwave and melt the dark chocolate.

3. Once the dark chocolate has fully melted, add the extra virgin olive oil to the microwaveable bowl and stir well with the wooden spoon.

4. Dip the Brazil nuts in the dark chocolate and ensure that each one is fully coated in dark chocolate.

5. After 2 hours, remove the baking tray from the refrigerator, place four Brazil nuts into each of the small plastic food bags and then grab a bag whenever you need a portable snack.

The Griddle Recipe Handbook

Salt & Pepper Pumpkin Seeds

These salt and pepper pumpkin seeds are a fantastic low carb alternative to chips and provide your body with plenty of copper, healthy fats, magnesium, manganese, phosphorus and protein.

What You'll Need:

- 2 tablespoons of extra virgin olive oil
- 2 teaspoons of black pepper
- 2 teaspoons of salt
- 1 cup of pumpkin seeds

Let's Griddle!

1. Prepare griddle for medium heat. Lightly oil.

2. Place the black pepper, extra virgin olive oil and salt into the mixing bowl and stir well with the wooden spoon.

3. Add the pumpkin seeds to the mixing bowl and stir them well with the wooden spoon until they are fully coated in the mixture.

4. Once the pumpkin seeds are fully coated, place on griddle.

5. Stirring frequently, 15 to 18 minutes, until golden brown.

6. Remove and let the salt and pepper pumpkin seeds cool for 1 hour.

7. After 1 hour, place four equal portions of salt and pepper pumpkin seeds into each of the four small plastic food bags and then grab a bag whenever you need a portable snack.

The Griddle Recipe Handbook

Maple Bacon Griddled Pumpkin

What You'll Need:

- ✓ Pumpkin, cut into 2x2 inch pieces
- ✓ 6 slices of bacon
- ✓ ½ cup all-purpose flour
- ✓ Salt and pepper to taste
- ✓ ½ brown sugar, if desired
- ✓ 1 tablespoon maple syrup, if desired

Let's Griddle!

1. Cook bacon as usual. Remove from heat, let cool. Crumble into small pieces.

2. Cut pumpkin into 2x2 inch cubes.

3. Place cubes in large bowl and season with salt, pepper and coat with flour.

4. Prepare griddle for medium heat. Lightly oil. Place pumpkin on griddle and cook, turning often until golden brown and tender.

5. Remove from heat, add bacon bits, let cool and serve.

6. If desired, place in large bowl. Mix with brown sugar, maple syrup until each piece is coated.

The Griddle Recipe Handbook

Dinner Recipes – Chicken, Pork and Steak

Lemon Pepper Marinated Pork

What You'll Need:

- Red onion sliced into rings
- Juice of 1 lemon
- 1 teaspoon ground black pepper
- Half a teaspoon chili powder
- Quarter cup soy sauce
- 2 cloves garlic chopped
- 1 tablespoon coconut sugar (or use 1 teaspoon honey)
- ½ to 1 lb. sukiyaki cut lean pork (any tender part)
- 1 tablespoon oil for frying
- Green onion for garnish

Let's Griddle!

1. In a bowl, combine the pork, soy sauce, lemon juice, chili powder, black pepper, coconut sugar, and garlic.

2. Mix everything together and let stand for 30 minutes in room temperature or up to overnight in the fridge.

3. Preheat griddle to medium heat and prepare with oil

4. Add the pork to your flat top. Cook both sides for about 2 minutes each, spoon the marinade or pork and cook until marinade dries up.

5. Add the red onion rings and sauté for about 2 more minutes.

6. Transfer to a serving dish.

7. Top with chopped green onions and serve with rice or just lettuce. Serves 2-4

The Griddle Recipe Handbook

Lemon Pepper Marinated Pork

What You'll Need:

- Red onion sliced into rings
- Juice of 1 lemon
- 1 teaspoon ground black pepper
- Half a teaspoon chili powder
- Quarter cup soy sauce
- 2 cloves garlic chopped
- 1 tablespoon coconut sugar (or use 1 teaspoon honey)
- ½ to 1 lb sukiyaki cut lean pork (any tender part)
- 1 tablespoon oil for frying
- Green onion for garnish

Let's Griddle!

1. In a bowl, combine the pork, soy sauce, lemon juice, chili powder, black pepper, coconut sugar, and garlic.

2. Mix everything together and let stand for 30 minutes in room temperature or up to overnight in the fridge.

3. Preheat griddle to medium heat and prepare with oil.

4. Add the pork to your flat top. Cook both sides for about 2 minutes each, spoon the marinade or pork and cook until marinade dries up.

5. Add the red onion rings and sauté for about 2 more minutes.

6. Transfer to a serving dish.

7. Top with chopped green onions and serve with rice or just lettuce. Serves 2-4

The Griddle Recipe Handbook

Honey Paprika Chicken Tenders Recipe

What You'll Need:

- 1 lb. chicken tenders, sliced into finger-thick slices
- Half a cup honey
- 1/3 cup dark soy sauce
- 3 tablespoons olive oil
- 1 tablespoon paprika
- 1 ½ to 2 tablespoons curry powder
- Salt and pepper to taste

Let's get the griddle ready for some honey paprika chicken tenders!

1. Preheat your griddle to medium-high.

2. Slice the chicken into half an inch-thick strips so they will cook faster and absorb more flavor.

3. In a bowl, combine the soy sauce, paprika, curry powder, honey, and olive oil.

4. Dump in the chicken and mix. Season with salt and pepper to taste.

5. Let the mixture stand for 10-15 minutes.

6. Place on griddle to cook half-way through.

7. Remove from flat top and transfer to a roasting pan and spread evenly so that the chicken pieces are just 1 layer.

8. Cover with aluminum foil and place roasting pan back on flat top until fully cooked through. Approximately 10 – 12 minutes.

9. Garnish with spring onion and enjoy!

10. This recipe serves 2-3 persons and the marinade/sauce can flavor up to 2 lbs. of chicken if cooking for more persons.

The Griddle Recipe Handbook

Sizzling Chicken Mushroom Recipe

What You Will Need:

- ½ pound chicken breast, cut into strips
- ½ cup button mushrooms, sliced
- ½ cup frozen green peas, thawed
- ½ cup water
- 1 tablespoon soy sauce
- A pinch of ground black pepper
- 1 heaping teaspoon cornstarch
- 1 teaspoon onion powder

Let's Get the Chicken Sizzling!

1. Make sure you got all of your ingredients ready to go.

2. Prepare your griddle to medium-high and place the chicken on it until cooked.

3. Add the mushrooms and the peas and cook for 3 minutes.

4. To make the sauce or the gravy, mix together the water, soy sauce, ground pepper, onion powder and cornstarch.

5. Place aluminum roasting pan on your flat top. Combine the chicken, mushrooms and peas mixture in roasting pan. It will thicken immediately. Stir for another 3 to 5 minutes. Take off the heat and serve.

6. The dish easily serves two persons and the recipe can be easily doubled to feed more. Enjoy!

The Griddle Recipe Handbook

Southern Fried Turkey Strips with Stuffed Mushrooms

What You'll Need:

- 4 * 4 oz. turkey steaks
- 4 large portabella mushrooms
- 1/3 cup extra virgin olive oil
- 2 tablespoons of tomato paste
- ½ cup of almonds
- 1 teaspoon of black pepper
- 1 teaspoon of cayenne pepper
- 1 teaspoon of paprika powder
- 1 teaspoon of salt
- ½ cup of shredded cheddar cheese

Let's Griddle!

1. Place the almonds, black pepper, cayenne pepper, paprika powder and salt into the food processor and blend until the almonds become fully powdered.

2. Once the almonds and other ingredients have become fully powdered, add them to the mixing bowl along with the extra virgin olive oil, then mix them together with the wooden spoon to form a marinade.

3. Once the marinade ingredients are fully mixed, add the turkey steaks to the mixing bowl and coat them fully in the marinade.

4. Once the turkey steaks are fully coated in marinade, pour them into the sealable container and put the container into the refrigerator for a minimum of 4 hours to allow the marinade to fully soak into the turkey steaks. If you have time, turn the turkey steaks halfway through to ensure that the marinade soaks into them evenly.

5. Prepare griddle for medium heat. Lightly oil. Place on chicken on griddle. Cover with basting cover. Add a little water to the surface before you cover. Until cooked through.

6. Spread an equal amount of tomato paste on the base of each portabella mushroom and then top with an equal amount of shredded cheddar cheese. Place on griddle, cover until cheese is melted.

7. Place one southern fried turkey steak and one stuffed portabella mushroom onto each of the four plates, serve and enjoy.

The Griddle Recipe Handbook

Orange-Cranberry Bone-In Chicken Breasts

What You'll Need:

- 2 T. coconut oil
- 2 lbs. bone-in chicken breasts, with skin
- 1½ t. fresh sage, chopped
- 1½ t. fresh thyme leaves
- Sea salt and black pepper, to taste
- ½ c. fresh (or frozen) cranberries
- 2 T. freshly squeezed orange juice
- 2 T. honey, preferably local
- ¼ t. ground cinnamon
- ½ t. ground ginger
- ¼ t. ground cloves
- 1/8 t. ground nutmeg

Let's Griddle!

1. Melt the coconut oil in a large, aluminum roasting pan over medium heat. Season the chicken with sage, and thyme. Season with salt and black pepper, to taste.

2. Prepare griddle for medium heat. Lightly oil. Place seasoned chicken in griddle skin-side down and cook until browned, approximately 4-5 minutes, or until it releases easily from the bottom of the pan. Turn the chicken and continue cooking another 4-5 minutes on the remaining side.

3. While the chicken is browning, add the cranberries, orange juice, honey, cinnamon, ginger, cloves, and nutmeg to a aluminum roasting pan. Place over medium heat and bring it to a gentle boil. Cook until the cranberries pop open and the sauce becomes slightly thickened, around 4-5 minutes.

4. Place chicken in roasting pan on your flat top. Cover and "roast" until the chicken is fully cooked through and the sauce is bubbly, around 15 to 20 minutes or until chicken is cooked through and reaches an internal temperature of 160°F.*

5. Remove from pan and transfer chicken to a serving platter. Cover loosely and let rest for 5 minutes before serving topped with the warm orange-cranberry pan sauce and your choice of sides. Enjoy!

*Internal temperature will continue to rise to 165°F as it rests.

The Griddle Recipe Handbook

Honey Applesauce Pork Roast

What You'll Need:

- 1 c. unsweetened applesauce
- 3 T. honey
- 2 T. sugar-free Dijon mustard
- 3 T. fresh rosemary leaves, chopped
- Sea salt and black pepper, to taste
- 2 T. coconut oil
- 1 lb. pork tenderloin
- 3 medium firm apples, cored and chopped

Let's Griddle!

1. Combine applesauce, honey, Dijon mustard, and rosemary leaves in a small bowl and stir to combine. Season with salt and black pepper, to taste, and set aside.

2. Melt the coconut oil in a large, aluminum roasting pan over medium heat. Generously season the pork roast with salt and black pepper, to taste.

3. Prepare griddle for medium-low heat. Lightly oil. Place on griddle. Cover with basting cover. Add a little water to the surface before you cover. Turning every 3 to 4 minutes. Cook time is approximately 15 minutes. Be careful not to allow any side to burn.

4. Remove from heat and spread half of the applesauce mixture all over the top and sides of the pork. Arrange the chopped apples around the sides of the pork and place in aluminum roasting pan. Increase heat to medium. Cover and roast for an additional 20 minutes.

5. After 10 minutes, flip the pork. Brush with remaining applesauce mixture and roast for another 10 minutes, or until the pork is cooked through.

6. Remove from oven and cover loosely to rest for 5 minutes before serving. Enjoy!

The Griddle Recipe Handbook

Steak

What You'll Need:

- 1 steak
- 1 salt
- 1 pepper

Let's Griddle!

1. This recipe is for any number of steaks including sirloin, T-bone, ribeye, etc.

2. Season your steak with salt and pepper, or any other seasoning of your choice.

3. Prepare griddle for medium-high heat. Lightly oil. Place steak on griddle.

4. When one side develops a crust, flip once. Until the steak is done to your desired doneness.

5. The most important point to remember when griddling a steak is to leave it alone. Let the juices, the seasoning and the heat make an excellent steak.

The Griddle Recipe Handbook

Herb-Rubbed, Bone-In Pork Chops

What You'll Need:

- 2 T. Kosher salt
- 6-8 large fresh basil leaves, torn into pieces
- 2 stems fresh rosemary, leaves stripped from stems and crushed
- 2 T. fresh thyme leaves, crushed with fingers
- 3 cloves garlic, smashed, peeled and roughly chopped
- 1 T. salt
- 4 thick-cut bone-in pork chops, approximately 1" thick

Let's Griddle!

1. Combine salt, basil, rosemary, thyme, garlic and pepper thoroughly in a small bowl. Rub mixture over all sides of pork chops until thoroughly covered.

2. Prepare griddle for medium heat. Lightly oil. Place on griddle. Cook for 7-8 minutes, turn once. Cover with basting cover. Add a little water to the surface before you cover. If your chops are thinner or thicker than 1", adjust cook time accordingly.

3. Remove chops from heat, cover and let rest for 3 - 5 minutes before serving. Serve with a summer vegetable medley and top with a pat of compound butter seasoned with the same herbs used in the rub.

The Griddle Recipe Handbook

Maple-Balsamic Boneless Pork Chops

What You'll Need:

- 1 T. extra virgin olive oil
- 4 4-oz. boneless pork chops
  Salt and black pepper, to taste
- ½ c. balsamic vinegar
- 2½ T. real maple syrup

Let's Griddle!

1. Prepare griddle for medium heat. Lightly oil.

2. Season pork chops on each side with salt and pepper, to taste, and add to the pre-heated griddle. Brown pork chops on each side, approximately 3 minutes per side. Remove pork chops from pan and set aside on a rimmed dish.

3. Place small aluminum roasting pan to your flat top. Heat this heat zone to high. Add balsamic vinegar and maple syrup and bring to a boil, stirring constantly.

4. Reduce heat to medium and cook mixture until it is reduced to about 1/3 of its original volume. When ready, the glaze will become thick and syrupy. (Do not overcook or the mixture will become hard and sticky).

5. Transfer chops to a serving platter or individual serving plate and drizzle with pan sauce. Serve immediately with griddled Brussels Sprouts or your choice of sides.

The Griddle Recipe Handbook

Kebab Recipes

Greek Salad Skewers

What You'll Need:

- 1 small organic cucumber, cut into 12 equally thick slices
- 8 oz. block Feta cheese, cut into 12 equal-size chunks
- 12 grape or cherry tomatoes, any color
  12 large black olives, pitted
- High-quality extra virgin olive oil, for drizzling
  ½ t. dried Italian seasoning
  Sea salt and black pepper, to taste

Let's Griddle!

1. Prepare griddle for medium heat. Lightly oil. Place cucumbers on flat top for 1 minutes. Turn to other side. Remove and let cool. This will as a crispy crunch to this dish. Arrange cucumber slices on a serving platter and top each with a chunk of Feta cheese.

2. Gently press the flat end of a wooden skewer through the cheese and cucumber until secure, then add a tomato, followed by a black olive to top each skewer.

3. Right before serving, drizzle extra virgin olive oil over the skewers and sprinkle with Italian seasoning. Season with salt and black pepper, to taste, and enjoy!

The Griddle Recipe Handbook

Chicken & Onion Kebabs

What You'll Need:

- ✓ 12 oz. of chopped chicken breast
- ✓ 2 tablespoons of extra virgin olive oil
- ✓ 2 tablespoons of lemon juice
- ✓ 2 tablespoons of white wine vinegar
- ✓ 1 clove of crushed garlic
- ✓ 1 chopped large onion
- ✓ 1 teaspoon of black pepper
- ✓ 1 teaspoon of dried basil
- ✓ 1 teaspoon of dried oregano
- ✓ 1 teaspoon of salt

Let's Griddle!

1. Add all the ingredients to the sealable container, stir well with the wooden spoon, seal the container and then refrigerate for a minimum of 4 hours to allow the ingredients to soak into the chicken breast and onion.

2. Remove the marinated chicken breast and onion from the refrigerator.

3. To prepare the kebabs, simply add chunks of chicken breast and onion to the wooden skewers in an alternating fashion

4. Prepare griddle for medium heat. Lightly oil. Place on griddle until on each side is fully cooked.

The Griddle Recipe Handbook

Pork & Red Pepper Kebabs

What You'll Need:

- 12 oz. of chopped pork
- 2 tablespoons of extra virgin olive oil
- 2 tablespoons of lemon juice
- 1 chopped large red bell pepper
- 1 teaspoon of dried basil
- 1 teaspoon of dried oregano
- 1 teaspoon of black pepper
- 1 teaspoon of salt

Let's Griddle!

1. Add all the ingredients to the sealable container, stir well with the wooden spoon, seal the container and then refrigerate for a minimum of 4 hours to allow the ingredients to soak into the pork and red pepper.

2. To prepare the kebabs, simply add chunks of pork and peppers to the wooden skewers in an alternating fashion

3. Prepare griddle for medium heat. Lightly oil. Place on griddle until on each side is fully cooked.

The Griddle Recipe Handbook

Monkfish & Mushroom Kebabs

What You'll Need:

- 12 oz. of chopped monkfish
- 4 chopped large mushrooms
- 2 tablespoons of lemon juice
- 2 tablespoons of lime juice
- 2 tablespoons of milk
- 1 clove of crushed garlic
- 1 teaspoon of black pepper
- 1 teaspoon of chili powder
- 1 teaspoon of ground ginger powder
- 1 teaspoon of salt

Let's Griddle!

1. Add all the ingredients to the sealable container, stir well with the wooden spoon, seal the container and then refrigerate for a minimum of 4 hours to allow the ingredients to soak into the monkfish and mushrooms.

2. To prepare the kebabs, simply add chunks of fish and mushrooms to the wooden skewers in an alternating fashion

3. Prepare griddle for medium heat. Lightly oil. Place on griddle until on each side is fully cooked.

The Griddle Recipe Handbook

Vegetable Kebabs

What You'll Need:

- 4 chopped large mushrooms
- 1 chopped large red pepper
- 1 chopped small summer squash
- 1 clove of crushed garlic
- 2 tablespoons of extra virgin olive oil
- 2 tablespoons of lemon juice
- 2 tablespoons of red wine vinegar
- 1 tablespoon of mustard
- 1 teaspoon of black pepper
- 1 teaspoon of dried basil
- 1 teaspoon of dried parsley
- 1 teaspoon of salt

Let's Griddle!

1. Add all the ingredients to the sealable container, stir well with the wooden spoon, seal the container and then refrigerate for a minimum of 4 hours to allow the ingredients to soak into the vegetables.

2. To prepare the kebabs, simply add chunks of vegetable to the wooden skewers in an alternating fashion

3. Prepare griddle for medium heat. Lightly oil. Place on griddle until on each side is fully cooked.

The Griddle Recipe Handbook

Healthy Fruit Kebabs

What You'll Need:

- ✓ 1 chopped medium mango.
- ✓ 1 chopped medium papaya.
- ✓ 1 chopped small melon.
- ✓ 1/2 chopped medium pineapple.

Let's Griddle!

1. Add all the chopped fruit to the sealable container, seal the container and then place it in the fridge until you are ready for the cookout.

2. To prepare the kebabs, simply add chunks of mango, melon, papaya and pineapple to the skewers in an alternating fashion, then grill them equally on each side until they're cooked.

The Griddle Recipe Handbook

Refreshing Drink Recipes

Watermelon Mint Lemonade

For an adults-only variation, *add some citrus-flavored vodka before serving.*

What You'll Need:

- Mint Simple Syrup (optional)
  ½ c. granulated sugar
- ½ c. water
  ¼ c. tightly packed fresh mint leaves, stems removed and crushed
- 6 c. fresh watermelon, rinds removed and cut into chunks
- ¾ c. fresh lemon juice (6-8 medium lemons)
- ½ c. cold water, (plus more, if needed)
- ½ c. fresh mint leaves, tightly packed with stems removed
- fresh mint sprigs, lemon slices, for garnish

Let's Enjoy a Refreshing Drink!

1. To make the simple syrup, add the sugar, water and crushed mint leaves to a small saucepan and heat over medium-high heat. Stir until the sugar dissolves completely. Reduce heat to low and simmer for 10 minutes. Remove from heat and discard mint leaves. Cool completely before using.

2. Add watermelon chunks, lemon juice and ½ cup cold water to a blender and blend until liquefied. Pour through a fine mesh strainer to remove any larger particles. Taste and add more water, if needed. Sweeten with mint-infused simple syrup, if desired.

3. Bruise ½ c. fresh mint leaves with fingers to release oils and add to the bottom of a large glass pitcher or jar. If serving immediately, add ice cubes to the container and pour the watermelon mixture over top. Add fresh lemon slices to the container for garnish. To serve, pour over ice and add a sprig of fresh mint and a lemon slice for garnish.

The Griddle Recipe Handbook

Sparkling Blackberry Basil Cocktail

What You'll Need:

- 8-10 large fresh or frozen blackberries
- 3 T. fresh basil, torn
- ¼ c. honey, preferably local
- ¼ c. water
- 4 oz. Elderflower liqueur (optional)
- 1 750 ml bottle Prosecco, chilled
- Garnish: (optional) Fresh blackberries, Sprigs of fresh basil

Let's Enjoy a Refreshing Drink!

1. Add the blackberries, basil, honey, and water to a small saucepan set over medium heat. Simmer, stirring occasionally, until mixture is heated through and starts to thicken, approximately 4-5 minutes. Gently press on blackberries while heating to release juices.

2. Remove from heat and strain mixture through a fine mesh strainer to remove solids. Reserve remaining liquid and set aside to cool.

3. If using, divide the Elderflower liqueur among four champagne flutes, along with a drizzle of the blackberry simple syrup. Finish by topping off each glass with some chilled Prosecco.

4. Garnish each glass with 2-3 fresh blackberries and a sprig of fresh basil, if desired, before serving. Enjoy!

The Griddle Recipe Handbook

Passion Tea Lemonade

What You'll Need:

- 5¼ c. water, divided
- 4 tea bags
- ¼ c. honey, preferably local
- 4" piece lemongrass, finely chopped
- 2 small cinnamon sticks
- ½ c. fresh lemon juice
- Ice, to serve
- Garnish: (optional) Fresh lemon slices and Sprigs of fresh mint

Let's Enjoy a Refreshing Drink!

1. Bring four cups water to a rapid bowl in a teapot or saucepan. Remove from heat and add tea bags.

2. To prepare the infused simple syrup, combine a quarter cup water, honey, lemongrass, and cinnamon sticks in a small saucepan and place over medium heat. Simmer, stirring occasionally, until mixture is heated through and starts to thicken, approximately 4-5 minutes.

3. Remove from heat and pour through a fine mesh strainer to separate the solids from the liquid. Discard solids and set the remaining simple syrup aside to cool.

4. Combine the brewed tea, lemon juice, and remaining cup of water in a large pitcher. Add infused simple syrup, to taste, and stir to combine.

5. To serve, fill four chilled glasses with ice before adding the sweetened iced tea mixture. Garnish with lemon slices and sprigs of fresh mint, if using, and serve immediately. Enjoy!

The Griddle Recipe Handbook

Cherry and Mint Fizz

What You'll Need:

- 2 c. dark cherries, pitted (fresh or frozen)
- 2 T. honey
- 1 c. water
- ¼ c. fresh lime juice
- 1 c. fresh mint leaves, washed, patted dry, and torn
- 2 c. club soda
- Optional Adults-Only Version: Add 1 oz. gin per serving

Let's Enjoy a Refreshing Drink!

1. Combine dark cherries, honey, and water in a small saucepan and place over medium heat. Cook, stirring frequently, for 4-5 minutes or until the mixture is warmed through and bubbly and the cherries release their juices.

2. Remove from heat and transfer the dark cherry mixture to a blender or food processor and blend until smooth. Pour into a pitcher and let cool at room temperature for 10-15 minutes.

3. Add lime juice and mint leaves and stir to combine. Place in the refrigerator until ready to serve.

4. To serve, fill four serving glasses with ice and add ¼ cup dark cherry mixture, ½ cup club soda, and one-ounce gin, if using, to each glass. Stir gently to combine and serve immediately. Enjoy!

The Griddle Recipe Handbook

Pink Grapefruit Martini – Adults Only

What You'll Need:

- Ice, to fill shaker
- 1½ c. fresh pink grapefruit juice
- ¼ c. fresh lime juice
- 6 oz. vodka
- 2 oz. orange liquor, such as Cointreau or triple sec
- 1 large lime, cut into slices

Let's Enjoy a Refreshing Drink!

1. Fill cocktail shaker with ice and add all other ingredients. Cover and shake vigorously to blend.

2. Remove lid and strain into martini glasses. Garnish with slices of lime and serve immediately. Enjoy!

The Griddle Recipe Handbook

Raspberry Margarita

What You'll Need:

- 1 ½ oz silver tequila
- 2 oz raspberry coulee
- 2 oz sweet & sour mix
- 1 oz simple syrup
- Sprite to fill glass
- Sugar to rim
- Ice

Let's Enjoy a Refreshing Drink!

1. Rim glass with simple syrup, and then edge it In the sugar. Mix all other ingredients and stir.

The Griddle Recipe Handbook

Asian Recipes

Beef Honey Curry Stir Fry Recipe

What You Will Need:

- Half a pound of sukiyaki cut beef
- Half a cup of honey
- Half a cup of soy sauce
- 4 tablespoons curry powder
- 4 tablespoons of oil
- 1 teaspoon ground black pepper
- 1 medium sized red onion, sliced
- 1 medium sized red bell pepper, sliced into strips
- 1 medium sized green bell pepper, sliced into strips
- 1 medium sized yellow bell pepper, sliced into strips
- Roasting pan

Let's Get Cooking!

1. Prepare all the ingredients that you'll need.

2. Marinate the beef with marinade made of soy sauce, curry powder, honey and ground black pepper and let it stand for 15 minutes.

3. Prepare your flat top to medium high heat. Oil and sauté the red bell pepper, green bell pepper, red onion and yellow bell pepper for a few minutes (usually just a little over a minute), taking care that the vegetables are cooked but not wilted. They should remain crunchy for great texture. Take the cooked vegetables off the pan and set aside.

4. Remove beef from marinate mixed and place on griddle until halfway cooked. Remove and place in roasting pan.

5. Place roasting pan on griddle and add in the remaining half of the oil and marinade and cook the beef together with the marinade over medium heat until the sauce thickens, and the beef is cooked through. This only takes 5-7 minutes. Turn off the heat.

6. Toss the cooked vegetables with the beef in the pain to coat it with some of the sauce and bring all flavors together. Serve over steaming hot rice, mashed potato, or even pasta! This recipe makes for about 3-4 servings.

The Griddle Recipe Handbook

Smoked Pork Sausage Hakka Noodles Recipe

What You Will Need:

- Hakka Noodles – 1 packet
- Smoked Pork Sausages - 5
- Coriander Leaves – 50gms
- Soya Sauce - 1 tbsp
- Mint Leaves – 50gms
- Onion – 1
- Green Chilies- 3
- Capsicum – 1
- Salt to Taste

Let's Get Cooking!

1. Cut and slice all the pork vegetables and keep it aside.

2. Then cook the packet of Hakka noodle in a container. Make sure to add a little bit of oil so that they don't stick together. Boil the noodles for 5-6 minutes.

3. Take the noodles and transfer them to a strainer and wash them under the tap so that they stop cooking.

4. Then add a little bit of oil and soya sauce to the noodles. Once this is ready, we are ready to cook the rest of the meal.

5. Prepare griddle for medium heat. Lightly oil. Add the onions and chilies till they turn light brown.

6. Then add the smoked pork sausages and cook it for 5 – 7 minutes.

7. Add the coriander and mint leaves and cook for another 5 minutes. The major aroma will be from the coriander and mint leaves.

8. Then add the cauliflower, capsicum and salt to taste.

9. Then add the noodles and then cook it for another 5 minutes.

10. Take it off the griddle and then serve it with mint leaves.

The Griddle Recipe Handbook

Asian Style Beef Broccoli Recipe

What You Will Need:

- ✓ Half a pound of sukiyaki cut beef (very thin across the grain slices)
- ✓ A bundle of Chinese broccoli (about 3 cups)
- ✓ 1/3 cup brown sugar
- ✓ 1/3 cup water
- ✓ 1/3 cup soy sauce
- ✓ 3 tablespoons cooking oil
- ✓ 2 tablespoons browned chopped garlic (you may use garlic flakes)
- ✓ 1-2 tablespoons sesame oil
- ✓ ½ teaspoon red chili flakes
- ✓ ½ teaspoon freshly grounded black pepper

Let's Heat Up the Kitchen!

1. Get all of your ingredients together.

2. Prepare griddle for medium heat. Lightly oil. Place on broccoli on flat top. Cover with basting cover. Add a little water to the surface before you cover to steam Chinese broccoli until it is done but not soggy. It is important to retain the bright green color for the visual appeal of the meal; plus the crunchy texture of the cooked vegetable add a certain freshness to the dish.

3. Cook the beef in the cooking oil until browned. It would only take 3 minutes in medium to high heat because the beef is very thinly cut.

4. Once the beef has been cooked and browned, add in the water, soy sauce, brown sugar, half of the garlic, the red chili flakes and black pepper. Simmer for 3 minutes.

5. On a serving dish, arrange the Chinese broccoli and spoon the cooked beef and the sauce over it. Top with the rest of the garlic flakes and drizzle in the sesame oil.

6. Serve and enjoy! This recipe serves 2-4 individuals depending if the dish is to be served as a side dish or a main dish. It's a visual treat for sure!

The Griddle Recipe Handbook

Exotic Asian Pork Burger Recipe

What You Will Need:

- One pound of ground pork
- 3 tablespoons vinegar (apple cider and white cane vinegar works well)
- 2-3 tablespoons brown sugar
- 1 teaspoon salt
- 1 whole head of garlic (crushed or grated)

Let's Start Burger Flipping!

1. Gather all the ingredients and measure out what you will need for the burger patties.

2. Combine everything thoroughly. The pork will get white from the vinegar because the acidity of the vinegar will slowly cure and cook the meat.

3. Form into patties (makes 4-8 patties, depending on size and thickness that you want). The patties can be frozen for up to 3 months and cooked when needed.

4. Prepare your griddle. Make smash burgers until thoroughly cooked.

5. Serve over your favorite bun with your choice of condiments and trimmings. As a suggestion, mustard and sriracha provides a great contrast to the tangy and garlicky flavor of the burger. Enjoy!

The Griddle Recipe Handbook

Oriental Glazed Pork

What You'll Need:

- ✓ 2 pounds pork with the bone left in (best cuts to use are shoulder or pork legs)
- ✓ 1-ounce piece of fresh ginger root, sliced thinly
- ✓ ½ cup soy sauce
- ✓ 1 tablespoon cooking oil
- ✓ ½ cup vinegar (cane vinegar or white wine vinegar works well)
- ✓ 2/3 cup water
- ✓ 1/3 cup brown sugar
- ✓ 2-3 pieces star anise

Let's Cook Up Some Juicy Glazed Pork!

1. Wash the pork pieces and place on griddle. Prepare griddle for medium-high and sear the pork pieces until some parts are fully browned. This technique gives the finished dish so much flavor!

2. Place aluminum roasting pan your flat top. Medium heat. Add 1 tablespoon olcive oil. Once the pork has been seared, add to pan although with the ginger slices and allow the ginger to infuse with the oil for about a minute.

3. Then add the soy sauce.

4. Followed by the water.

5. And then the vinegar. Cover and cook on medium heat until only about half a cup of the liquid remains.

6. Add in the sugar and star anise. Make sure the sugar gets dissolved in the sauce. Coat the pork pieces with this mixture and then cover. Simmer for about 2 to 3 minutes until you can really smell the aromatic flavor of the star anise.

7. The finished dish will be glossy, delicious, and oh-so-tempting!

8. Serve with plenty of rice. This dish is good for 4 to 6 generous servings.

The Griddle Recipe Handbook

Pot Stickers

What You'll Need:

- 1-pound lean pork mince
- 1 small head Napa cabbage shredded or cut into slaw-size pieces (about 2 cups)
- 1 teaspoon sesame oil (optional)
- Dumpling wrappers (about 30-36 pieces, exactly 1 packet from the store)
- 1 cup green onion, cut into very small pieces
- 1 teaspoon salt
- Pepper to taste (just a pinch to be on the safe side)
- Half a cup of water per cooking batch
- 1 teaspoon oil per cooking batch

Let's Make Some Delicious Dumplings!

1. Cook the pork mince halfway through. Remove and let cool. Then in a bowl, combine the pork mince, Napa cabbage, salt, pepper, sesame oil, and green onions. Mix everything together thoroughly until you can make balls out of the mixture and the balls stay formed. Let the mixture rest for about half an hour.

2. When you're ready to make dumplings, place about a tablespoon of the mixture in the center of a dumpling wrapper. Wet the edges with a bit of water and fold over to seal the edges together.

3. To create the dumpling shape, press the dumpling's rounded side down. Repeat until you've gone through all your mixture and dumpling wrappers (you will be able to make about 30-36 dumplings).

4. To cook, place dumplings on your flat top. Lightly oil griddle top. Cook covered over medium high heat. dd a little water to the surface before you cover. The steam will cook the dumplings thoroughly.

5. After about 10 minutes, take off the cover. The water will dry up and the bottoms of the dumplings will start to fry from the rendered pork fat and the oil. Perfectly crisp dumpling bottoms!

6. Repeat steps 8 and 9 to cook the rest. You can also freeze the uncooked dumplings on a tray until frozen and then transfer into separate ziplock bags for 'instant' pan-fried dumplings when you feel like having them.

The Griddle Recipe Handbook

Sweet & Sour Pork Chops with Peppers & Pineapple

What You'll Need:

- 2 T. extra virgin olive oil, divided
- 4 boneless pork chops, approximately 1/2" thick
- Sea salt and black pepper, to taste
- ¼ c. balsamic vinegar
- ¼ c. real maple syrup
- 3-4 garlic cloves, minced
- 2 t. dried rosemary, chopped
- ½ t. crushed red pepper flakes
- 1 red bell pepper, sliced thin
- 1 yellow bell pepper, sliced thin
- 2 c. fresh pineapple chunks
- 3 large green onions, diced
- ¼ c. fresh parsley, chopped

Let's Griddle!

1. Prepare griddle for medium-high heat. Lightly oil. Add the pork chops and sear on both sides, approximately 1-2 minutes per side. Season with salt and black pepper, to taste, on each side while cooking.

2. Place aluminum roasting pan on flat top. Heat to medium. Combine the vinegar, maple syrup, garlic, rosemary, and red pepper flakes in pan. Season with salt and black pepper, to taste, and cook, stirring occasionally, until slightly thickened, approximately 4-5 minutes. Reduce heat to low and continue to simmer, stirring occasionally, until ready to serve.

3. Meanwhile, add the sliced peppers to the flat top and sear over medium-high heat. Season with salt and black pepper, to taste. Cook, stirring occasionally, until the peppers soften and develop a bit of color, approximately 6-8 minutes.

4. Add the pineapple and continue cooking until heated through, approximately 2-3 minutes. Stir in the green onion and parsley and remove from heat.

5. Plate pork chops and pour the glaze over the pork chops and serve alongside the peppers and pineapple. Enjoy!

The Griddle Recipe Handbook

How to Make Super Juicy and Flavorful Hamburgers

There are two things you need for super juicy, flavorful burgers: Fat and seasonings. For the best tasting burgers, choose ground meat with a higher fat content.

For example, pick regular ground beef instead of ground chuck, ground round or ground sirloin. If the package labeling doesn't clearly indicate what you are buying, don't be afraid to ask the person behind the meat counter to point you in the right direction.

On its own, ground beef doesn't have much flavor, so it is important to add additional seasoning. For this recipe, a combination of sweet Italian pork sausage, salt, pepper, Worcestershire sauce, onion, garlic and fresh rosemary are used to pack a lot of flavor into each bite.

As an added bonus, the Worcestershire sauce and onion increase the juiciness of the burger without adding a lot of extra fat.

The Griddle Recipe Handbook

Super Juicy Grilled Burgers with Blue Cheese and Avocado

What You'll Need:

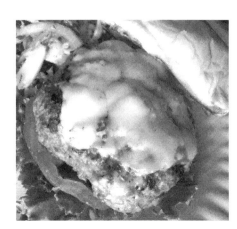

- 2 lbs. regular ground beef
- 1 lb. sweet Italian pork sausage
- 3 T. Worcestershire sauce
- ¼ c. white onion, very finely minced or grated
- 4 cloves garlic, very finely minced or grated
- 3 T. fresh rosemary, stems removed and leaves finely minced
- salt and pepper, to taste
- Optional toppings: lettuce, tomato slices, blue cheese, sliced avocado and bacon

Let's Griddle!

1. Add all ingredients to a large glass bowl and combine thoroughly. Make sure both types of meat and all seasonings are completely incorporated throughout the mixture.

2. Divide meat mixture into 8 equal parts and shape each part into ¾ inch thick patties. Place patties on medium heated griddle and smash. Cook until desired doneness.

3. If topping with soft, sliced cheese, add slices about one minute before cooking is complete. If using a harder, chunky cheese, such as blue cheese, move burgers to non-heated zone. Top with blue cheese and cover to allow cheese to melt completely.

4. Serve on toasted buns with lettuce, tomato, slices of avocado and bacon, if desired – or top with your favorite condiments, instead.

The Griddle Recipe Handbook

Chicken Burgers

What You'll Need:

- 12 oz. ground chicken breast
- 2 tablespoons of onion powder
- 1 teaspoon of black pepper
- 1 teaspoon of cayenne pepper
- 1 teaspoon of extra virgin olive oil
- 1 teaspoon of salt
- 1/2 cup of milk
- 1/2 cup of whole wheat breadcrumbs

Let's Griddle!

1. Add the black pepper, cayenne pepper, extra virgin olive oil, ground chicken breast, milk, onion powder, salt and a quarter of the whole wheat breadcrumbs to the large mixing bowl and stir well with the wooden spoon.

2. Once all the ingredients are fully mixed into the ground chicken, form four patties on the chopping board.

3. Coat each patty with the remaining whole wheat breadcrumbs, place all four in the sealable container and refrigerate until you are ready for the cookout.

4. Prepare your griddle and cook to desired doneness.

The Griddle Recipe Handbook

Super Duper Juicy Hamburgers

What You'll Need:

- 12 oz. ground beef
- 2 large eggs
- 1 shredded medium onion
- 1 teaspoon of black pepper
- 1 teaspoon of salt
- 1/4 cup of whole wheat breadcrumbs

Let's Griddle!

1. Add all the ingredients to the large mixing bowl and stir well with the wooden spoon.

2. Once all the ingredients are fully mixed into the ground beef, form four patties on the chopping board.

3. Place all four patties in the sealable container and refrigerate until you are ready for the cookout.

4. Prepare your griddle and cook to desired doneness.

The Griddle Recipe Handbook

Lamb Burgers

What You'll Need:

- 12 oz. ground lamb
- 2 large eggs.
- 1 teaspoon of black pepper
- 1 teaspoon of mint sauce
- 1 teaspoon of salt
- 1/4 cup of whole wheat breadcrumbs

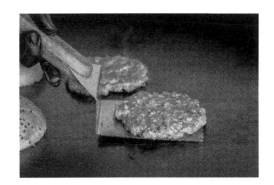

Let's Griddle!

1. Add all the ingredients to the large mixing bowl and stir well with the wooden spoon.

2. Once all the ingredients are fully mixed into the ground lamb, form four patties on the chopping board.

3. Place all four patties in the sealable container and refrigerate until you are ready for the cookout.

4. Prepare your griddle and cook to desired doneness.

The Griddle Recipe Handbook

Salmon Burgers

What You'll Need:

- 12 oz. finely chopped salmon
- 2 large eggs
- 1 medium onion
- 1 teaspoon of dried basil
- 1 teaspoon of dried thyme
- 1 teaspoon of lemon juice
- 1 teaspoon of lime juice
- 1/4 cup of whole wheat breadcrumbs

Let's Griddle!

1. Add all the ingredients to the blender and blend until everything is combined but not completely puréed.

2. Remove the mixture from the blender and form four patties on the chopping board.

3. Place all four patties in the sealable container and refrigerate until you are ready for the cookout.

4. Prepare your griddle and cook to desired doneness.

The Griddle Recipe Handbook

Vegetable Burgers

What You'll Need:

- ✓ 2 large eggs.
- ✓ 1 clove of crushed garlic.
- ✓ 1 shredded small carrot.
- ✓ 1 shredded small onion.
- ✓ 1 shredded small summer squash.
- ✓ 1 tablespoon of extra virgin olive oil (15ml).
- ✓ 1 tablespoon of soy sauce (15ml).
- ✓ 1/4 cup of porridge oats (39g).
- ✓ 0.5 oz. cheddar cheese (15g).
- ✓ 1/2 cup of whole wheat breadcrumbs (30g).

Let's Griddle!

1. Add the extra virgin olive oil, carrot, garlic, onion and summer squash to the griddle on medium heat for 5 minutes.

2. After 5 minutes, remove and pour the ingredients into the large mixing bowl.

3. Add the cheddar cheese, egg, oats and soy sauce to the large mixing bowl and stir well with the wooden spoon.

4. Once all the ingredients are fully mixed, form four patties on the chopping board.

5. Coat each patty with the whole-wheat breadcrumbs, place all four in the sealable container and refrigerate until you are ready for the cookout.

6. Prepare your griddle and cook to desired doneness.

The Griddle Recipe Handbook

Tex Mex Sliders

What You'll Need:

- 3 tbsp. *Traverse Bay Farms Chunky Salsa*
- 1/3 c. breadcrumbs
- 1 ½ lbs. lean ground beef
- 6 slices Pepper Jack cheese, halved
- 12 Pre-baked dinner rolls or mini buns
- Extra salsa as condiment

Let's Griddle!

1. In large bowl, combine beef, salsa and breadcrumbs. Form into 12 small patties. Place on griddle over medium heat until insides are no longer pink and juices run clear.

2. Top burgers with Pepper Jack cheese. Cover until cheese is melted.

3. Assemble sliders, adding extra salsa in place of traditional condiments.

The Griddle Recipe Handbook

Turkey Spinach Burgers

What You'll Need:

- 12 oz ground turkey
- 1 small box frozen spinach
- ½ cup diced onion, optional
- ½ cup diced celery
- ½ tsp poultry seasoning
- 1 tsp garlic salt
- ½ tsp black pepper
- ¼ cup sunflower seeds
- Breadcrumbs

Let's Griddle!

1. Thaw and drain the spinach squeezing out the excess moisture. Mix the turkey, spinach, sunflower seeds and seasonings together.

2. Add enough breadcrumbs to make the mixture hold together. Divide into patties griddle over medium heat until desired doneness is reached. Serve on a bun or perhaps over rice with brown gravy.

The Griddle Recipe Handbook

Mexican Recipes

Goat Cheese Quesadilla Recipe

What You Will Need:

- ✓ Flour tortillas (this recipe uses 12-inch diameter flour tortillas)
- ✓ 1 small red bell pepper, cut into strips
- ✓ 1 small green bell pepper, cut into strips
- ✓ 3-4 ounces of goat cheese

Let's Flip Some Quesadillas!

1. Get everything you need ready and set to go.

2. Preheat to medium heat and slightly oil, heat up both sides of the flour tortilla.

3. Place the red and green bell peppers, and the goat cheese on one side of the flour tortilla.

4. Fold the flour tortilla in half and place under melting dome or cover under aluminum foil. Flip until both sides are browned and the cheese have melted.

5. Cut the quesadilla in manageable wedges and serve with hot sauce and mustard for filling meal. This recipe serves two for snack portions and 1 for dinner. What's great is that you may substitute the goat cheese for mozzarella or other mild cheese, making this dish totally customizable and convenient!

The Griddle Recipe Handbook

Chimichangas (Shredded Beef)

What You Will Need:

- 4 (12 inch) flour tortillas
- 8 cups precooked shredded beef
- 4 avocados, skinned and seeded
- 1 cup sour cream
- 2 pickled jalapeno chiles, seeded and minced
- 2 tablespoons juice from the pickled jalapeno chilies
- 1/4 cup cilantro, minced

Let's Griddle!

1. In a food processor, add two of the skinned, seeded avocados, sour cream, chiles, chili juice and cilantro. Process until thick and smooth.

2. Thinly slice the remaining two avocados & divide into 4 servings.

3. Place tortillas on griddle. Medium-low heat.

4. Place 2 cups shredded beef and one serving of sliced avocado to each tortilla.

5. Fold and griddle tortillas until crispy.

6. Plate and top with avocado sauce.

The Griddle Recipe Handbook

Ancho Chicken Quesadillas

What You Will Need:

- 12 oz. shredded rotisserie or griddled chicken breast
- 1 T. ancho chili powder
- 2 cloves garlic, finely minced
- 2 T. fresh lime juice
- 1 tsp ground cumin
- 2 T. extra virgin olive oil
- 1 tsp red pepper flakes
- 1 tsp salt
- 1 tsp black pepper
- 4 extra-large flour tortillas (or 8 smaller ones)
- 12 oz. shredded Mexican cheese mix (can substitute with a mixture of cheddar and Monterey Jack), plus a little extra for garnish, if desired.
- 2 T. fresh cilantro, stems removed and coarsely chopped.
- 1 T. fresh cilantro, stems removed and coarsely chopped, for garnish

Let's Griddle!

1. Place shredded chicken in a medium glass bowl. Combine chili powder, garlic, lime juice, cumin, olive oil, red pepper flakes, salt and pepper in a separate bowl, then pour over shredded chicken. Toss to coat thoroughly.

2. Heat griddle to medium heat and add one tortilla. For extra-large tortillas, place 1/4 of the seasoned chicken on one side (for smaller tortillas, cover the entire surface). Layer 3 oz. of shredded cheese on top and 1/2 T. of chopped fresh cilantro. Fold over remaining side of tortilla (or place a second smaller one on top) and gently flip over once the bottom tortilla is nicely browned.

3. Gently press on top of tortilla after flipped for better contact with flat top and to help melt the cheese inside. Continue cooking until second side is browned, as well.

4. Remove from griddle and cover to keep warm while repeating the process the remaining ingredients. To serve, top each warm tortilla with a little shredded cheese and fresh cilantro. Delicious with salsa and guacamole, if desired.

The Griddle Recipe Handbook

Easy Chicken Quesadillas

What You Will Need:

- 2 tablespoons extra virgin olive oil
- 1 small or ½ medium onion, finely minced
- 2 cloves fresh garlic, finely minced
- ½ cup chicken broth or water
- 2 tablespoons taco seasoning mix
- 1 teaspoon salt
- 1 teaspoon pepper
- 2 tablespoons butter
- 8 10" flour tortillas
- 2 cups pre-cooked chicken, shredded (rotisserie works great)
- 2 cup shredded white cheese (Monterey Jack or Pepper Jack)
- 1 bunch fresh cilantro, stems removed and finely chopped.
- 2 jalapeno peppers, seeded and diced – optional
- **Serve with Traverse Bay Farms Red Raspberry salsa - optional**

Let's Griddle!

1. Add extra virgin olive oil and onion to griddle. Heat over medium-high heat until onion becomes translucent, about 6 - 8 minutes. Add garlic and stir for 1 - 2 minutes or until it starts to turn brown.

2. Plan roasting pan on flat top. Heat to medium-high. Add chicken broth, taco seasoning, salt and pepper to pan. Stir until dry ingredients are completely dissolved.

3. Add shredded chicken to the pan and toss to coat in the seasonings. Turn heat to medium-low and simmer until any excess moisture is absorbed.

4. Remove from heat and keep warm.

5. Place one tortilla on griddle. Top with ½ cup seasoned shredded chicken mixture and ½ cup shredded cheese. Add fresh cilantro and diced jalapeno peppers, if desired.

6. Distribute ingredients evenly and place second tortilla on top. Carefully flip once the bottom tortilla turns golden brown. Once both sides are browned and cheese is melted, remove from heat and slice into 8 wedges. Serve immediate with fresh salsa, guacamole, sour cream or pico de gallo.

The Griddle Recipe Handbook

Tequila Lime Beef Tacos

What You Will Need:

- ✓ 2 pounds of hamburger
- ✓ 3 TBSP oil
- ✓ Salt, pepper, garlic powder, onion powder, chili powder, cumin – lightly sprinkled over roast
- ✓ 1 – 4oz can mild diced green chiles
- ✓ 1 – 14.5oz Fire Roasted Diced Tomatoes – Salsa Style (or substitute one can regular fire roasted diced tomatoes plus ½ cup of your favorite salsa)
- ✓ 3 TBSP good silver tequila
- ✓ 2 tsp chile powder
- ✓ Soft taco shells
- ✓ Juice of 1 lime
- ✓ Toppings of your choice

Let's Griddle!

1. Prepare griddle for medium heat. Lightly oil. Cook hamburger as you would normally. Remove from heat and place in bowl.

2. Combine meat with green chiles, chili powder, other ingredients and fire roasted tomatoes (and salsa if you are using it), tequila and stir. Place back on griddle and cooking for 2 minutes.

3. Heat taco shells on griddle.

4. Immediately before serving, stir in the juice of 1 lime into the beef.

The Griddle Recipe Handbook

Pizza Recipes

BBQ Chicken Pizza

What You Will Need:

- 1 medium sized unfrozen or homemade pizza crust
- 1 cup of *Traverse Bay Farms Cherry BBQ sauce*
- 1.5 cups cooked grilled or roasted chicken, homemade or from the deli, sliced into cubes
- 1.5 cups shredded smoked mozzarella or regular mozzarella
- 1 large red onion, cut into rings or half rings

Let's Make Some Mean BBQ Chicken Pizza!

1. Preheat the griddle to low and gather everything you need.

2. Mix up the sliced chicken with the BBQ sauce.

3. To help the pizza crust not get soggy, griddle the crust by itself for 5 minutes until it is just starting to be lightly browned.

4. Place the chicken and sauce mixture over the baked pizza crust, making sure to spread everything as evenly as you can.

5. Sprinkle half the mozzarella on top of the chicken and sauce mixture.

6. Load up the red onions.

7. Top with the rest of the cheese.

8. Place bake on griddle and cover with aluminum foil. Cook for 10 minutes or until the pizza has browned and the cheese has fully melted. Rotate the pizza to ensure it doesn't burn.

9. This recipe can easily serve 2-3 people as a full meal. Enjoy.

The Griddle Recipe Handbook

Breakfast Pizza

What You Will Need:

- ✓ 2 eggs
- ✓ 10-12 inch flour tortilla (in this recipe we used the whole wheat variety)
- ✓ 2 ounces of shredded cheese (cheddar is a good option, as is mozzarella)
- ✓ 3 pieces sun dried tomatoes preserved in oil, chopped
- ✓ 2 slices of regular bacon (or 1 round of Canadian bacon), chopped
- ✓ 1-2 hash brown patties, crumbled

Let's Make Some Pizza!

1. Cook the hash brown patties on your flat top. Medium heat and lightly oiled. Remove and crumble into small pieces.

2. Cook the scrambled eggs. Remove.

3. Lower your griddle to low heat. Lay down the flour tortilla and spread the cheese and bacon over it.

4. Follow it up with the sun-dried tomatoes and the hash brown crumbles. Distribute evenly.

5. Evenly distribute the scrambled eggs and cheese.

6. Cover with aluminum foil for 5 to 7 minutes until the toppings are cooked, the cheese is fully melted, and the tortilla crust has crisped up.

7. Serve up! This makes for a hearty breakfast for one or can be shared with someone. Enjoy!

The Griddle Recipe Handbook

Caprese Pizza with Tortilla Crust

What You Will Need:

- 1/3 to ½ cup marinara sauce or tomato sauce (can use tomato puree)
- 1 10-12 inch whole wheat flour tortilla (may use regular tortilla)
- ½ teaspoon dried oregano (1 teaspoon if using fresh leaves)
- Some basil leaves
- 3-4 ounces of mozzarella cheese
- Ground black pepper (to taste)
- Dried red chili flakes (optional)

Pizza Time!

1. Make your own no-cook pizza sauce by combining the marinara, tomato sauce, tomato puree, ground black pepper, red chili flakes and oregano leaves together.

2. Spread the sauce over the top of the whole wheat tortilla. Layer in some basil leaves and crumble/shred the mozzarella on top.

3. Cover with aluminum foil for 5 to 7 minutes until the toppings are cooked, the cheese is fully melted, and the tortilla crust has crisped up.

4. You may drizzle in some olive oil if you want, but this pizza with a twist is good as it is.

5. Enjoy this simplified pizza!

The Griddle Recipe Handbook

Oregano Pizza Crust Recipe

What You'll Need:

- 1 packet of instant dry yeast
- 1 tablespoon dry oregano (use 2 tablespoons if using fresh leaves)
- 1 tablespoon sugar
- 3 tablespoons olive oil
- 2 teaspoons coarse salt (only 1 teaspoon for fine salt)
- 3 ½ cup bread flour (or use all-purpose flour)
- 1 and 1/3 cup warm water

Let's Make Some Homemade Pizza Crust!

1. Bring out all your ingredients.

2. Begin by blooming the yeast. In your bowl, mix the water, sugar, and yeast. The mixture will give a faint yeasty aroma after 3-5 minutes of being mixed.

3. In another bowl, combine the flour, oregano and salt.

4. Combine the flour and yeast mixture.

5. You may use a hand mixer or a stand mixer with a dough attachment. You can also do this step manually by using a big spoon to combine the ingredients together.

6. Knead and mix until well combined, which should be at about 3-5 minutes using a mixer and 10-15 minutes or more by hand. Take out the dough and coat the bottom the bowl with olive oil.

7. Place the dough in the bowl and turn it over once, thereby coating the whole dough ball with olive oil. Place in a warm place lightly covered with a kitchen towel for about 30 minutes to an hour until the dough doubles in size.

8. Once the dough has risen, punch it down and roll into a bowl again.

9. Prepare a flat working surface by dusting it with flour.

10. At this point, you may use everything to make individual pizzas.

11. When cooking, cook each side for a few minutes until slightly brown. This will prevent the dough from getting soggy. Place your topping. Cook in low heat, covered with aluminum foil until cheese is melted.

The Griddle Recipe Handbook

Seafood Recipes

Sausage & Shrimp Recipe

What You'll Need:

- ✓ 2 cups cooked rice, use whatever kind you prefer
- ✓ 1 cup shrimp
- ✓ Half a cup frozen peas
- ✓ ½ lb. your favorite spicy sausage, sliced
- ✓ 3-4 cups chicken stock or seafood stock depending on which you prefer and how much water your rice needs to cook
- ✓ 1 red onion, roughly chopped
- ✓ Half a tablespoon of dried oregano
- ✓ Salt and pepper to taste

Let's Griddle!

1. Preheat griddle to medium high. Prepare with oil. Place sausage on your griddle until browned.

2. Add in the chopped onion to your flat top and sauté until the onion becomes translucent.

3. Add to your flat top the cooked rice and oregano. Stir until the rice is coated with the oil from the sausage and oil. Remove and place in bowl.

4. Place roasting pan on griddle. Add the chicken broth, rice, sausage, shrimp and peas. No more stirring from this point. Reduce to medium. Cover with aluminum foil for 10 minutes. Season with salt and pepper to taste.

5. Voila! A delicious and gorgeous dinner for 3-4 persons! Best served with some chili oil and a slice of lemon. Enjoy!

The Griddle Recipe Handbook

Smoked Salmon Rollups Recipe

What You'll Need:

- 12-inch flour tortilla (we are using whole wheat flour tortillas in this recipe)
- 1 tablespoon mayonnaise
- 1 tablespoon mustard
- Toothpicks or cocktail skewers
- 3 ounces of smoked salmon, sliced thinly
- A few leaves of lettuce (either iceberg or romaine)
- 3 slices of mild cheese (the one used for sandwiches)

Time to Roll up Some Appetizers!

1. Get all of your ingredients ready.

2. Spread the mayonnaise and the mustard over a rectangular area of the flour tortilla.

3. Add in the lettuce.

4. Add a layer of smoked salmon.

5. Then a layer of cheese. Arranging them this way will create a nice color contrast when you cut the roll up into slices.

6. Roll the tortilla tightly, secure with toothpicks/cocktail skewers about an inch apart. Place on griddle preheated to low heat. Turn until all sides are brownish. Remove and let cool.

7. Use this as a cutting/slicing guide. Cut the rolled-up tortilla using a very sharp knife.

8. This recipe is for a single roll which makes 10-12 slices.

9. You may serve this for brunch, cocktails, or even dinner! Enjoy!

The Griddle Recipe Handbook

Warm Garlic-Parmesan Shrimp

What You'll Need:

Garlic-Parmesan Shrimp What You'll Need:

- 3 T. extra virgin olive oil
- 3-4 cloves garlic, finely minced
- 2 t. Dijon mustard
- 1 t. ground cumin
- 3 T. Parmesan cheese, freshly grated
- Sea salt and black pepper, to taste
- 1½ lbs. jumbo shrimp, peeled and deveined
- 1½ T. lemon juice
- 1/3 c. fresh parsley, minced
- Will also need: Parchment paper

Let's Griddle!

1. Prepare griddle for medium heat. Lightly oil. Place garlic on griddle until done. Remove and let cool.

2. Prepare the garlic shrimp seasoning by combining the olive oil, minced garlic, Dijon mustard, ground cumin, and grated Parmesan cheese in a large glass or other non-reactive bowl. Season with salt and black pepper, to taste.

3. Add shrimp to the bowl and toss to combine. Transfer the seasoned shrimp to a preheated griddle to low heat 3 to 4 minutes, or until the shrimp are just firm and pink. Do not overcook.

4. Remove shrimp and sprinkle with lemon juice and fresh parsley. Toss to combine when just cool enough to handle. Serve immediately. Enjoy!

The Griddle Recipe Handbook

Lemon-Garlic Jumbo Shrimp

What You'll Need:

- 3 T. unsalted butter
- 1 T. garlic, finely minced
- 1 lb. Jumbo shrimp (10/15 ct.), peeled, deveined, and tail removed
- 1 large organic lemon, zest and juice
  1 T. ground cumin
- Optional: Salt and pepper, to taste
- Fresh parsley leaves, chopped

Let's Griddle!

1. Prepare griddle for medium heat. Lightly oil. Add garlic and sauté for 1-2 minutes, stirring occasionally.

2. Add shrimp and cook for 4-5 minutes, stirring occasionally, or until shrimp starts to turn pink.

3. Add lemon zest, dash of lemon juice, and ground cumin and combine thoroughly. Season with salt and black pepper, to taste, and remove from heat. Serve immediately and enjoy!

The Griddle Recipe Handbook

Grilled Tequila Shrimp

What You'll Need:

- 2 pounds of large, unpeeled shrimp
- ½ cup of peanut oil (olive oil can be used instead)
- ½ cup of Tequila, any brand
- ¼ cup of lime juice
- 2 shallots, chopped
- 2 medium cloves of garlic, minced
- 2 teaspoons of ground cumin
- Salt and Pepper

Let's Griddle!

1. If you are using wooden skewers, be sure to soak them in water for an hour before you get started.

2. Thread 3 or 4 shrimp onto the skewers and place them all in a shallow glass dish. Don't use an aluminum pan!

3. In a bowl, mix the tequila, lime juice, garlic, shallots, cumin, and salt and pepper. Base the salt and pepper on your personal taste. Slowly whisk in the peanut oil until everything is well blended. Pour over the shrimp and leave in the refrigerator for 2 to 4 hours to marinate.

4. Oil the griddle and bring the grill to medium heat. Lay out the skewers and cook for about 3 or 4 minutes on each side. Serve immediately.

5. Note: Waste not-Want not! Use the remaining tequila to make a cocktail called Tequila Sunrise. The original recipe called for tequila, cream de cassis, lime juice and soda water but a more popular version uses tequila, orange juice, and grenadine syrup. It gets its name from the way it looks after pouring into a glass. To make 4 drinks, mix 8 measures of tequila with 8 dashes of grenadine and add orange juice.

The Griddle Recipe Handbook

Orange Roughie with Oven-Roasted Tomatoes

What You'll Need:

- 4 orange roughy filets
- 4 oven-dried tomato slices
- 4 fresh or preserved lemon slices, cut in half
  2 T. fresh thyme
- 4 T. unsalted butter
- salt and pepper, to taste

Let's Griddle!

1. Place a filet on prepared griddle on low heat. Place 1 large oven-dried tomato slice and 2 lemon slice halves on top of each. Top each filet with ¼ of the fresh thyme and add 1 T. of butter. If desired, sprinkle with salt and pepper, to taste.

2. Cover with basting dome. Add a little water to the surface before you cover. The goal is to steam and lightly cook the fish.

3. Cook for about 8 - 10 minutes. Add a couple minutes to your cooking time if starting with frozen filets.

4. To serve, discard lemon slices. Transfer filets to plates.

The Griddle Recipe Handbook

Steamed Citrusy Orange Roughie

What You'll Need:

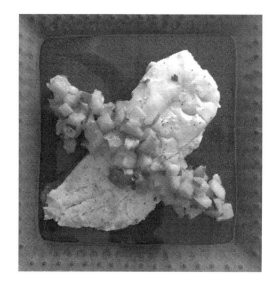

- 4 orange roughie filets
- 12 slices fresh or salt-cured preserved lemon
- 8 slices fresh lime
- 2 T. fresh cilantro, stems removed and chopped
- 1 T. fresh jalapeno pepper, seeds and veins removed and finely chopped
- 4 T. unsalted butter
- salt and pepper, to taste

Let's Griddle!

1. Place a filet on prepared griddle on low heat. Add 3 lemon slices and 2 lime slices on top of each. Top each filet with ¼ of the cilantro and jalapeno pepper. Top with 1 T. of butter and sprinkle with salt and pepper, to taste.

2. Cover with basting dome. Add a little water to the surface before you cover. The goal is to steam and lightly cook the fish.

3. Cook for about 8 - 10 minutes. Add a couple minutes to your cooking time if starting with frozen filets.

4. To serve, discard lemon slices. Transfer filets to plates.

The Griddle Recipe Handbook

Coconut Shrimp with Avocado-Lime Dip

What You'll Need:

- ½ c. almond (or coconut) flour
- 1 t. smoked paprika
- 1 t. ground cumin
- 1 t. garlic powder
- 1 t. onion powder
- Sea salt and black pepper, to taste
- 2 eggs
- 2 T. water
- ¾ c. shredded coconut, unsweetened
- 1 lb. 10/15 count gulf shrimp, peeled and deveined, tails on

Avocado Lime Dip:

- 1 large ripe avocado, pitted and peeled
- 3 T. fresh cilantro, stems removed
- 2 T. fresh lime juice
- ¼ t. ground cumin
- ½ t. red pepper flakes
- Sea salt and black pepper, to taste

Let's Griddle!

1. Combine almond flour, smoked paprika, ground cumin, garlic powder, and onion powder in a pie pan or shallow bowl. Season with salt and black pepper, to taste, and set aside. In a second pie pan or shallow bowl, gently whisk the eggs and water until frothy. Season with salt and black pepper, as desired, and set aside.

2. Add shredded coconut to a third bowl and set aside. Working one at a time, dredge each shrimp in the seasoned almond flour, then dip in the egg mixture. Allow excess egg to drip off before transferring shrimp to the bowl of shredded coconut. Turn to coat shrimp thoroughly before transferring to the prepared baking sheet. Repeat with remaining shrimp and season with additional salt and black pepper, if desired.

3. Place on prepared griddle with low heat. Until golden-brown and crispy, around 4 to 6 minutes, turning once halfway through. Meanwhile, add avocado, cilantro, lime juice, and cumin to a food processor or blender and blend until smooth. Add a tablespoon or two of water, if necessary, to reach desired consistency. Season with salt and black pepper, to taste. Transfer to a small serving bowl and sprinkle with red pepper flakes. Serve immediately. Enjoy!

The Griddle Recipe Handbook

Citrus Jumbo Scallops

What You'll Need:

- 1 butter -- as needed, melted
- 1 fresh parsley --, chopped
- 12 jumbo scallops --, halved

Sauce

- 1 c water
- 1/4 lemon -- juiced
- 1 c chardonnay wine
- 1 T butter
- 2 t honey
- 1 pn salt
- 1/2 clove garlic -- diced
- 1 cup cornstarch -- dissolved in water

Let's Griddle!

1. In small saucepan, combine water, wine, juice, butter, honey with peppers and garlic. Place over medium heat; reduce to almost half, stirring frequently. Add cornstarch solution to thick to taste. Remove from heat; keep warm.

2. Griddle scallops, brushing frequently with melted butter. Cook to taste. Remove scallops from griddle. Place 6 scallop halves on each plate. Pour citrus sauce over scallops and garnish with parsley.

The Griddle Recipe Handbook

Tofu Recipes

Crispy Buffalo Tofu Fingers

What You'll Need:

- 1 block firm tofu, drained and cut into half-inch thick sticks
- 1 tablespoon potato flour (or use cornstarch)
- Half a teaspoon table salt
- 1 teaspoon fine ground black pepper
- 3 tablespoons butter (use margarine if vegan)
- Quarter cup your favorite hot sauce
- Green onion for garnish
- oil for frying the tofu

Let's Griddle!

1. Begin by seasoning the tofu with salt and pepper and sprinkling potato flour over it.

2. Lightly toss the tofu in the potato flour.

3. Preheat griddle to medium high, oil the griddle and place the tofu on the griddle.

4. Make sure all sides are browned.

5. Drain the tofu on paper towels.
6.
7. In separate bowl, combine the melted the butter and hot sauce.

8. Mix together and stir to make sure it does not burn. Turn off the heat.

9. Quickly toss the tofu in the sauce.

10. Transfer unto a plate, sprinkle with green onions, and serve immediately. Good for 2 people.

The Griddle Recipe Handbook

Garlic Tofu and Beans Stir Fry

What You'll Need:

- 2 cups fresh green beans, sliced into 2-inch long sections
- 1 block firm tofu, sliced into half-inch thick slabs
- 2 tablespoons soy sauce
- Cayenne pepper to taste
- 2 cloves garlic
- 2 tablespoons soybean oil or canola oil
- 1 cup vegetable stock
- Half a teaspoon ground black pepper
- Oil

Let's Griddle!

1. Preheat your griddle to medium high. Add oil and place tofu slices until golden brown. Drain on paper towels and slice into half-inch thick strips.

2. Place aluminum roasting pan on your flat top. Bring heat to medium-high. Mix bean and vegetable stock. Remove beans and place on griddle. Cook until halfway done. Reserve a quarter cup of the stock for later.

3. When you have used up about ¾ of the stock, add the soybean oil and garlic. Sauté until garlic is fragrant.

4. Season with black pepper and stir-fry for half a minute.

5. Add the soy sauce and toss until soy sauce is nearly gone.

6. Toss in the tofu.

7. Add the last of the vegetable stock and keep stirring to coat the beans and tofu with the 'sauce'.

8. Transfer to a serving dish and garnish with cayenne to taste.
   Serves 2 as main dish and 4 as side dish.

The Griddle Recipe Handbook

Korean Spicy Braised Tofu

What You'll Need:

- 1 block firm tofu, drained and sliced into half inch-thick square
- 1-2 tablespoon Korean red pepper flakes (do not substitute other red pepper flakes!)
- Oil for prepping your griddle
- 1 tablespoon canola or soybean oil
- 1 small red onion chopped finely or 2 tablespoons shallots
- 2 cloves garlic, chopped finely
- 1 cup vegetable broth
- ½ teaspoon salt
- 1 tablespoon soy sauce
- 1 tablespoon brown sugar
- Toasted sesame seeds for garnish
- Extra Korean red pepper flakes for garnish

Let's Griddle!

1. Preheat griddle to medium-high. Place on griddle until the tofu until golden on both sides, drain excess oil on paper towels.

2. Place roasting pan on griddle. Increase heat to medium high, sauté the onion and garlic with the soybean oil until onion is translucent.

3. Add the broth, Korean red pepper flakes, sugar, soy sauce, and salt.

4. Mix everything until dissolved and add the tofu.

5. Lower heat to medium and simmer the tofu in the sauce for about 10 minutes, turning every few minutes.

6. Once the liquid is nearly gone, turn off the heat. Sprinkle with additional red pepper flakes if desired. Garnish with toasted sesame seeds.

7. Transfer unto a plate.

8. Enjoy! Serves 2.

The Griddle Recipe Handbook

Teriyaki Tofu Steaks

What You'll Need:

- ✓ 1 block firm tofu, drained and sliced into half-inch thick steaks
- ✓ Oil
- ✓ 2 cloves garlic, chopped finely
- ✓ 1 small red onion, chopped finely
- ✓ Quarter cup soy sauce
- ✓ 2 tablespoons mirin
- ✓ Quarter cup water
- ✓ 1 tablespoon agave syrup (or use 1.5-2 tablespoons sugar)
- ✓ Green onion for garnish

Let's Griddle!

1. Preheat griddle to medium heat.

2. Place tofu on flat top until golden on both sides.

3. Remove and place on paper towel.

4. Place roasting pan on flat top. Add oil and add both the garlic and the onion.

5. Follow with the soy sauce, water, mirin, and agave syrup.

6. Allow the sauce to reduce, turning the tofu every 2 minutes.

7. Once the sauce is slightly thickened and only a few tablespoons are left, the dish is done.

8. Transfer unto a plate or over some steamed rice.

9. Garnish with some green onion.
   Serves 2-3.

The Griddle Recipe Handbook

Salad Recipes

Making healthy salads is totally a work of art. Salads include a variety of different ingredients and flavors in them, which contribute to gourmet eating in a way. Salads may include meat or can be made without meat as well, they can be fluffed up with many things in no time, and seriously speaking, they are considered among the best healthy foods.

Enjoy these great tasting and simple salad recipes to enjoy with your griddle masterpieces.

Caesar Salad

What You'll Need:

- 2 cloves of garlic.
- 2 tablespoons of mustard (30ml).
- 2 teaspoons of mayonnaise (10ml).
- 2 teaspoons of white wine vinegar (10ml).
- 2 teaspoons of Worcester sauce (10ml).
- 1 head of shredded romaine lettuce.
- 1/2 cup of yogurt (118ml).
- 1/4 cup of parmesan (25g).
- Pinch of black pepper.
- Pinch of salt.

Let's Make a Great Salad!

1) Place the parmesan cheese and garlic in the blender and blend until they are finely chopped.

2) Add the black pepper, mustard, mayonnaise, salt, white wine vinegar, Worcester sauce and yogurt to the blender and blend until the mixture reaches the desired consistency (this usually takes about 30 seconds).

3) Add the Romaine lettuce to the sealable container, pour the blended mixture on top, stir well with the wooden spoon, seal the container and then refrigerate for a minimum of 4 hours to allow the Caesar dressing to fully soak into the romaine lettuce.

4) When it's time for the cookout, remove the healthy Caesar salad from the refrigerator. If you are attending a cookout, simply bring the sealed container with you. If you are hosting a cookout, simply transfer the healthy Caesar salad to the large bowl and serve it to your guests with the large serving spoon.

The Griddle Recipe Handbook

Coleslaw

What You'll Need:

- ✓ 4 tablespoons of yogurt
- ✓ 1 chopped small onion
- ✓ 1 shredded medium carrot
- ✓ 1 tablespoon of mayonnaise
- ✓ 1 tablespoon of mustard
- ✓ 1/2 shredded small white cabbage
- ✓ Pinch of black pepper.
- ✓ Pinch of salt.

Let's Make a Great Salad!

1) Add all the ingredients to the sealable container, stir well with the wooden spoon, seal the container and then refrigerate for a minimum of 4 hours to allow the mayonnaise, mustard and yogurt to soak into the vegetables.

2) When it's time for the cookout, remove the healthy coleslaw from the refrigerator. If you are attending a cookout, simply bring the sealed container with you. If you are hosting a cookout, simply transfer the healthy coleslaw to the large bowl and serve it to your guests with the large serving spoon.

The Griddle Recipe Handbook

Green Pea Salad

What You'll Need:

- ✓ 3 cups of cooked green peas
- ✓ 1 chopped medium red bell pepper
- ✓ 1 shredded medium carrot
- ✓ 1 teaspoon of black pepper
- ✓ 1 teaspoon of dried dill
- ✓ 1 teaspoon of dried oregano
- ✓ 1 teaspoon of dried parsley
- ✓ 1 teaspoon of garlic powder
- ✓ 1 teaspoon of onion powder
- ✓ 1 teaspoon of salt
- ✓ 3/4 cup of cottage cheese
- ✓ 1/4 cup of milk

Let's Make a Great Salad!

1) Place the black pepper, cottage cheese, dill, parsley, garlic powder, milk, onion powder, oregano powder and salt in the blender and blend until smooth.

2) Add the cooked green peas, medium carrot and red bell pepper to the sealable container, pour the blended mixture on top, stir well with the wooden spoon, seal the container and then refrigerate for a minimum of 4 hours to allow the dressing to fully soak into the vegetables.

3) When it's time for the cookout, remove the healthy green pea salad from the refrigerator. If you are attending a cookout, simply bring the sealed container with you. If you are hosting a cookout, simply transfer the healthy green pea salad to the large bowl and serve it to your guests with the large serving spoon.

The Griddle Recipe Handbook

Ranch Salad

What You'll Need:

- 4 cups of shredded iceberg lettuce
- 1 cup of halved cherry tomatoes
- 1 teaspoon of black pepper
- 1 teaspoon of dried dill
- 1 teaspoon of dried parsley
- 1 teaspoon of garlic powder
- 1 teaspoon of onion powder
- 1 teaspoon of salt
- 3/4 cup of cottage cheese
- 1/4 cup of milk

Let's Griddle!

1) Place the black pepper, cottage cheese, dill, parsley, garlic powder, milk, onion powder, oregano powder and salt in the blender and blend until smooth.

2) Add the cherry tomatoes and iceberg lettuce to the sealable container, pour the blended mixture on top, stir well with the wooden spoon, seal the container and then refrigerate for a minimum of 4 hours to allow the dressing to fully soak into the vegetables.

3) When it's time for the cookout, remove the healthy ranch salad from the refrigerator. If you are attending a cookout, simply bring the sealed container with you. If you are hosting a cookout, simply transfer the healthy ranch salad to the large bowl and serve it to your guests with the large serving spoon.

The Griddle Recipe Handbook

Sweet Potato Salad

What You'll Need:

- 1 cooked & chopped large sweet potato
- 1 chopped medium onion
- 1/2 chopped medium cucumber
- 1/2 cup of sour cream
- 1/4 cup of yogurt
- 1 tablespoon of extra virgin olive oil
- 1 tablespoon of mayonnaise
- Pinch of black pepper
- Pinch of salt

Let's Make a Great Salad!

1) Add all the ingredients to the sealable container, stir well with the wooden spoon, seal the container and then refrigerate for a minimum of 4 hours to allow the dressing to fully soak into the vegetables.

2) When it's time for the cookout, remove the healthy sweet potato salad from the refrigerator. If you are attending a cookout, simply bring the sealed container with you. If you are hosting a cookout, simply transfer the healthy sweet potato salad to the large bowl and serve it to your guests with the large serving spoon.

The Griddle Recipe Handbook

Marinated Strip Steak Salad with Creamy Blue Cheese Dressing

What You'll Need:

Strip Steak:

- ✓ 2 10-oz. strip steaks
- ✓ 1 T. kosher salt
- ✓ 3 T. olive oil, divided
- ✓ 3 T. Worcestershire sauce
  3 large garlic cloves, peeled, smashed, and roughly chopped
- ✓ 4 sprigs fresh rosemary, leaves removed and crushed

Salad:

- ✓ 2 small heads Bibb lettuce, base removed, leaves washed and dried
- ✓ 12 oz. roasted golden beets and purple potatoes, cut into equal-sized small chunks
- ✓ 4 oz. good quality blue cheese

Creamy Blue Cheese Dressing:

- ✓ ¼ c. full fat sour cream
- ✓ ¼ c. The Ojai Cook Lemonaise*
- ✓ 2 t. Worcestershire sauce
  ½ medium shallot, outer skin removed and very finely minced
  2 oz. chunky blue cheese
- ✓ 2-3 T. half & half
- ✓ Sea salt and freshly cracked pepper, to taste

*Can substitute an equal amount of mayonnaise and 1 tablespoon fresh lemon juice if you can't find this ingredient. (Amazon link included below)

The Griddle Recipe Handbook

Let's Griddle!

1. For best results, sprinkle the steaks with kosher salt on both sides and place in the refrigerator overnight.

2. The next day, combine 1 tablespoon olive oil, Worcestershire sauce, garlic and rosemary in a non-reactive bowl large enough to hold both steaks. Add salted steaks to the bowl and turn to coat. Place in refrigerator for at least 2 hours, turning occasionally.

3. Remove steaks from the refrigerator at least 30 minutes before cooking to allow them to reach room temperature. This will ensure they cook more evenly.

4. Prepare griddle for medium-high heat. Lightly oil. Place on griddle. Cook steaks to desired doneness.

5. When done, remove steaks and transfer to a platter. Cover with aluminum foil and allow to rest for at least 5 minutes. Remove cover and allow to cool slightly before slicing. Set aside.

6. To make the blue cheese dressing, add the first 4 ingredients to a medium glass or non-reactive bowl and stir to combine. Add the blue cheese and use a fork to break up the chunks and incorporate the cheese into the mixture. (If you prefer a chunkier dressing, leave some of the chunks intact).

7. Add the half & half one tablespoon at a time to the bowl until you reach the desired consistency. Add more half & half if you prefer a less thick dressing. Season with salt and pepper, to taste. Set aside.

8. To assemble the salad, place Bibb lettuce on 4 plates and add 1/4 of the roasted beets, potatoes, and blue cheese chunks to each plate. Divide sliced steak and add to each plate before drizzling with creamy blue cheese dressing. Serve immediately with sea salt and fresh cracked black pepper.

The Griddle Recipe Handbook

Great Tasting Salad Dressings

Caesar Dressing

Equipment Required:

- ✓ 1 Blender
- ✓ 1 Medium Bowl (if you are hosting a cookout)
- ✓ 1 Sealable Container (if you are attending a cookout)

What You'll Need:

- ✓ 2 Cloves of Garlic
- ✓ 2 Tablespoons of Mustard
- ✓ 2 Teaspoons of Mayonnaise
- ✓ 2 Teaspoons of White Wine Vinegar
- ✓ 2 Teaspoons of Worcester Sauce
- ✓ 1/2 Cup of Yogurt
- ✓ 1/4 Cup of Parmesan
- ✓ Pinch of Black Pepper
- ✓ Pinch of Salt

Let's Make a Great Salad!

1. Place the parmesan cheese and garlic in the blender and blend until they are finely chopped.

2. Add the black pepper, mustard, mayonnaise, salt, white wine vinegar, Worcester sauce and yogurt to the blender and blend until it reaches the desired consistency (this usually takes about 30 seconds).

3. If you are hosting a cookout, pour the mixture into a medium bowl, ready to serve to your guests. If you are attending a cookout, pour the mixture into a sealed container, ready to bring with you.

The Griddle Recipe Handbook

Ranch Dressing

Equipment Required:

- ✓ 1 Blender
- ✓ 1 Medium Bowl (if you are hosting a cookout)
- ✓ 1 Sealable Container (if you are attending a cookout)

What You'll Need:

- ✓ 1 Teaspoon of Black Pepper
- ✓ 1 Teaspoon of Dried Dill
- ✓ 1 Teaspoon of Dried Parsley
- ✓ 1 Teaspoon of Garlic Powder
- ✓ 1 Teaspoon of Onion Powder
- ✓ 1 Teaspoon of Salt
- ✓ 3/4 Cup of Cottage Cheese
- ✓ 1/4 Cup of Milk

Let's Make a Great Salad!

1. Place all the ingredients in the blender and blend until smooth.

2. If you are hosting a cookout, pour the mixture into a medium bowl, ready to serve to your guests. If you are attending a cookout, pour the mixture into a sealed container, ready to bring with you.

The Griddle Recipe Handbook

Blue Cheese Dressing

Equipment Required:

- ✓ 1 Medium Bowl (if you are hosting a cookout)
- ✓ 1 Large Bowl
- ✓ 1 Sealable Container (if you are attending a cookout)
- ✓ 1 Whisk
- ✓ 1 Wooden Spoon

What You'll Need:

- ✓ 3 Cloves of Finely Chopped Garlic
- ✓ 2 Tablespoons of White Wine Vinegar
- ✓ 1 Tablespoon of Mustard
- ✓ 1 Teaspoon of Black Pepper
- ✓ 1 Teaspoon of Salt
- ✓ 1/4 Cup of Blue Cheese Crumbles
- ✓ 1/4 Cup of Buttermilk
- ✓ 1/4 Cup of Sour Cream

Let's Make a Great Salad!

1. Place the black pepper, buttermilk, chopped garlic, mustard, salt, sour cream and white wine vinegar in the large bowl and whisk until smooth.

2. Add the blue cheese crumbles to the large bowl, mash it in with the wooden spoon and then stir until the blue cheese crumbles until they dissolve into the mixture.

3. If you are hosting a cookout, pour the mixture into a medium bowl, ready to serve to your guests. If you are attending a cookout, pour the mixture into a sealed container, ready to bring with you.

The Griddle Recipe Handbook

Tomato Ketchup

Equipment Required:

- ✓ 1 Medium Bowl (If you are hosting a cookout)
- ✓ 1 Large Bowl
- ✓ 1 Medium Saucepan
- ✓ 1 Sealed Container
- ✓ 1 Wooden Spoon

What You'll Need:

- ✓ 3 Teaspoons of Sugar
- ✓ 1 Can of Tomato Pastes
- ✓ 1 Teaspoon of Garlic Powder
- ✓ 1 Teaspoon of Onion Powder
- ✓ 1 Teaspoon of Salt
- ✓ 1/2 Cup of Cider Vinegar

Let's Griddle!

1. Place the saucepan on the hob on a low heat and add all the ingredients.

2. Stir continuously with the wooden spoon until the mixture starts to simmer.

3. Once the mixture starts to simmer, stir continuously for a further 5 minutes.

4. Remove the saucepan from the hob and turn off the heat.

5. Pour the mixture from the saucepan into the large bowl and leave it to cool for 1 hour.

6. After 1 hour, pour the mixture into a sealed container and place it in the refrigerator to cool for a further hour or until you are ready for the cookout.

7. Once you are ready for the cookout, take the sealed container out of the refrigerator. If you are attending a cookout, simply bring this container with you. If you are hosting a cookout, pour the mixture from the container into a medium bowl, ready to serve to your guests.

The Griddle Recipe Handbook

Sausage Recipes

Sausages are another cookout favorite that taste good but are generally high in calories and filled with processed ingredients. When you add to this the fact that many sausages are served as hot dogs with calorie rich bread rolls and condiments, they're not the healthiest of choices.

These five healthy cookout sausage recipes cut the calories and the processed ingredients, leaving you with a leaner, tastier sausage that will help you keep the weight off all summer long.

The Griddle Recipe Handbook

Pork Sausages

These healthy pork sausages pack a real punch and are much more appealing than most processed sausages. If you find them too spicy, simply use less cayenne pepper.

Equipment Required:

- 1 large mixing bowl
- 1 sausage stuffer
- 1 sealable container
- 1 small bowl
- 1 wooden spoon

What You'll Need:

- 12 oz. of ground pork
- 2 cups of cold water
- 1 meter of natural sausage casing
- 1 teaspoon of black pepper
- 1 teaspoon of cayenne pepper
- 1 teaspoon of ground sage
- 1 teaspoon of salt

Let's Make Some Great Sausage!

1. Add the cold water and sausage casing to the small bowl and leave the sausage casing to soften for about 30 minutes.
2. While the sausage casing is softening, add all the other ingredients to the large mixing bowl and stir well with the wooden spoon.
3. Once all the ingredients are fully mixed into the ground pork and the sausage casing is fully softened, stuff the mixture into the sausage casing using sausage stuffer.
4. Form the stuffed casing into four separate sausage links and tie the ends off.
5. Place the four-sausage links in the sealable container and refrigerate until you are ready for the cookout.
6. When it's time for the cookout, remove the healthy pork sausages from the refrigerator. If you are attending a cookout, simply bring the sealed container with you and then cook them directly on the grill when you get there. If you are hosting a cookout, simply cook them directly on your own grill.
7. To keep the pork sausages healthy and low in calories, don't eat them with bread, cheese or condiments. Instead, enjoy them with a portion of any of the healthy salads discussed earlier in this cookbook.

The Griddle Recipe Handbook

Beef Sausages

Equipment Required:

- 1 large mixing bowl
- 1 sausage stuffer
- 1 sealable container
- 1 small bowl
- 1 wooden spoon

What You'll Need:

- 12 oz. of ground beef
- 2 cups of cold water
- 1 meter of natural sausage casing
- 1 teaspoon of black pepper
- 1 teaspoon of garlic powder
- 1 teaspoon of onion powder
- 1 teaspoon of salt

Let's Make Some Great Sausage!

1. Add the cold water and sausage casing to the small bowl and leave the sausage casing to soften for about 30 minutes.
2. While the sausage casing is softening, add all the other ingredients to the large mixing bowl and stir well with the wooden spoon.
3. Once all the ingredients are fully mixed into the ground beef and the sausage casing is fully softened, stuff the mixture into the sausage casing using sausage stuffer.
4. Form the stuffed casing into four separate sausage links and tie the ends off.
5. Place the four sausage links in the sealable container and refrigerate until you are ready for the cookout.
6. When it's time for the cookout, remove the healthy beef sausages from the refrigerator. If you are attending a cookout, simply bring the sealed container with you and then cook them directly on the grill when you get there. If you are hosting a cookout, simply cook them directly on your own grill.
7. To keep the beef sausages healthy and low in calories, don't eat them with bread, cheese or condiments. Instead, enjoy them with a portion of any of the healthy salads discussed earlier in this cookbook.

The Griddle Recipe Handbook

Lamb Sausages

These healthy lamb sausages are soft, tender and pack have a refreshing, minty twist. If you're a fan of the lamb burgers from earlier in this cookbook, you'll love these.

Equipment Required:

- 1 large mixing bowl
- 1 sausage stuffer
- 1 sealable container
- 1 small bowl
- 1 wooden spoon

What You'll Need:

- 12 oz. of ground lamb
- 2 cups of cold water
- 1 meter of natural sausage casing
- 1 teaspoon of black pepper
- 1 teaspoon of mint sauce
- 1 teaspoon of salt

Let's Make Some Great Sausage!

1. Add the cold water and sausage casing to the small bowl and leave the sausage casing to soften for about 30 minutes.
2. While the sausage casing is softening, add all the other ingredients to the large mixing bowl and stir well with the wooden spoon.
3. Once all the ingredients are fully mixed into the ground lamb and the sausage casing is fully softened, stuff the mixture into the sausage casing using sausage stuffer.
4. Form the stuffed casing into four separate sausage links and tie the ends off.
5. Place the four-sausage links in the sealable container and refrigerate until you are ready for the cookout.
6. When it's time for the cookout, remove the healthy lamb sausages from the refrigerator. If you are attending a cookout, simply bring the sealed container with you and then cook them directly on the grill when you get there. If you are hosting a cookout, simply cook them directly on your own grill.
7. To keep the lamb sausages healthy and low in calories, don't eat them with bread, cheese or condiments. Instead, enjoy them with a portion of any of the healthy salads discussed earlier in this cookbook.

The Griddle Recipe Handbook

Turkey Sausages

These healthy turkey sausages have a lighter, less powerful taste and are a fantastic choice if you prefer a milder flavored sausage.

Equipment Required:

- ✓ 1 large mixing bowl
- ✓ 1 sausage stuffer
- ✓ 1 sealable container
- ✓ 1 small bowl
- ✓ 1 wooden spoon

What You'll Need:

- ✓ 12 oz. of ground turkey
- ✓ 1 clove of crushed garlic
- ✓ 1 meter of natural sausage casing
- ✓ 1 tablespoon of extra virgin olive oil
- ✓ 1 teaspoon of black pepper
- ✓ 1 teaspoon of dried thyme
- ✓ 1 teaspoon of ground sage
- ✓ 1 teaspoon of salt

Let's Make Some Great Sausage!

1. Add the cold water and sausage casing to the small bowl and leave the sausage casing to soften for about 30 minutes.
2. While the sausage casing is softening, add all the other ingredients to the large mixing bowl and stir well with the wooden spoon.
3. Once all the ingredients are fully mixed into the ground turkey and the sausage casing is fully softened, stuff the mixture into the sausage casing using sausage stuffer.
4. Form the stuffed casing into four separate sausage links and tie the ends off.
5. Place the four-sausage links in the sealable container and refrigerate until you are ready for the cookout.
6. When it's time for the cookout, remove the healthy lamb sausages from the refrigerator. If you are attending a cookout, simply bring the sealed container with you and then cook them directly on the grill when you get there. If you are hosting a cookout, simply cook them directly on your own grill.
7. To keep the turkey sausages healthy and low in calories, don't eat them with bread, cheese or condiments. Instead, enjoy them with a portion of any of the healthy salads discussed earlier in this cookbook.

The Griddle Recipe Handbook

Vegetable Sausages

Healthy vegetable sausages are another brilliant option for vegetarians or people who want to go meatless. This tasty recipe combines bread, cheese and a range of shredded vegetables for a super tasty, highly nutritious sausage.

Equipment Required:
- 1 chopping board
- 1 frying pan
- 1 large mixing bowl
- 1 sealable container
- 1 wooden spoon

What You'll Need:

- 2 large eggs
- 2 shredded large mushrooms
- 1 clove of crushed garlic
- 1 cup of whole wheat breadcrumbs
- 1/2 cup of shredded cheddar cheese
- 1 shredded medium onion
- 1 tablespoon of extra virgin olive oil
- 1 teaspoon of black pepper
- 1 teaspoon of dried parsley
- 1 teaspoon of salt

Let's Make Some Great Sausage!

1. Add the black pepper, dried parsley, extra virgin olive oil, garlic, mushrooms, onion, salt and half of the whole-wheat breadcrumbs to the frying pan, place it on the hob on a medium heat and fry for 5 minutes.
2. After 5 minutes, take the frying pan off the hob and pour the ingredients into the large mixing bowl. Add the cheddar cheese and eggs to the large mixing bowl and stir well with the wooden spoon. Once all the ingredients are fully mixed, form four sausage shaped patties on the chopping board.
3. Coat each patty with the remaining whole wheat breadcrumbs, place all four in the sealable container and refrigerate until you are ready for the cookout.
4. When it's time for the cookout, remove the healthy vegetable sausages from the refrigerator. If you are attending a cookout, simply bring the sealed container with you and then cook them directly on the grill when you get there. If you are hosting a cookout, simply cook them directly on your own grill.
5. To keep the vegetable sausages healthy and low in calories, don't eat them with bread, cheese or condiments. Instead, enjoy them with a portion of any of the healthy salads discussed earlier in this cookbook.

The Griddle Recipe Handbook

Additional Resources:

Traverse Bay Farms

Traverse Bay Farms has won 30+ national food awards at America's largest and most competitive food competition. They have a complete selection of nationally award-winning barbecue sauce, salsa, mustards and more. **www.TraverseBayFarms.com**

BeerBrewingVideos.com

If you like to homebrew, this site is for you. Updated daily with homebrewing information, videos and more. **BeerBrewingVideos.com**

Please note, if you have a copy of the first edition of this recipe book, two of the companies mentioned in the resource section are no longer in business.

Made in the USA
Coppell, TX
15 April 2020